SPACE CAREERS

Leonard David and Scott Sacknoff

With a Foreword by
BUZZ ALDRIN

International Space Business Council LLC
Bethesda, Maryland

Space Careers

Leonard David and Scott Sacknoff
With a Foreword by Buzz Aldrin

Published by:
International Space Business Council LLC
P.O. Box 5752
Bethesda, MD 20824-5752
United States
Phone: +1 (703) 524-2766
Email: career@spacebusiness.com
Website: www.spacebusiness.com/careers

Original Edition: First Printing 1998, Second Printing 1999
Fully Revised and Updated Edition: 2015

Printed in the United States of America
Book Cover Design: Gary Milgrom
Photo Credits: Clockwise from left: Atlas rocket (NASA), Astronaut Joe Allen with "For Sale" sign modified by author (NASA), Ground Control (NASA), *Maven* prior to launch (NASA KSC), ISS (ESA artist impression), Mission Control (NASA), center/*Thor 7* satellite (SSL).

ISBN: 978-1-887022-19-4 (Trade Paper)
ISBN: 978-1-887022-20-0 (e-book)

10 9 8 7 6 5 4 3 2

Table of Contents

About the Authors

Leonard David is a space journalist who has reported on space activities for more than 45 years. Winner of the National Space Club Press Award in 2010, Leonard has served as editor-in-chief of the National Space Society's *Ad Astra*, *Space World*, and *Final Frontier* magazines as well as being a featured contributor to publications such as *Space News*, SPACE.com, *Aerospace America*, *Sky and Telescope*, and *Aviation Week & Space Technology*.

He has consulted with NASA, other government agencies and the aerospace community and served as director of research for the National Commission on Space, a U.S. Congress/White House study that appraised the next 50–100 years of space exploration. In 2013, he coauthored, with Gemini and *Apollo 11* astronaut Buzz Aldrin, the National Geographic book *Mission to Mars—My Vision for Space Exploration*.

Additionally, along with his wife, Barbara David, he has worked on a number of educational outreach programs developing materials that focus on space-related science projects. For more on Leonard, please visit: www.leonarddavid.com.

Scott Sacknoff began his career as a project engineer, developing and testing next generation Space Shuttle engine components before becoming a consultant where he focused on the commercial and business side of the industry. For more than twenty years he performed varied commercial space consulting studies and analyses for NASA, DoD, and private sector contractors as well as working in venture capital, as an entrepreneur, and in the investment sector. Today, he serves as the publisher of the history journal, *Quest: The History of Spaceflight* (www.spacehistory101.com) and manages the SPADE Defense Index (NYSE: DXS), an investment benchmark focused on defense, space, and national security www.spadeindex.com. He is an alumnus of Rensselaer Polytechnic Institute (RPI) and of the International Space University.

Acknowledgments

We would like to offer special thanks to the following people for their help with this publication:

- **Barbara David,** for acting as a sounding board and providing input on content.

- **Marillyn Hewson,** Chairman, President, and CEO of Lockheed Martin, for offering her insight to job seekers regarding how to improve their résumés and interview skills

- **Eileen Kropf,** a College and Career Center specialist at the Thomas Jefferson High School for Science and Technology (Alexandria, Virginia), for providing us insight from a high school perspective.

- **Jennifer Walters,** Rensellaer Polytechnic Institute's director of the Center for Career and Professional Development, for providing us with insight from a university perspective.

- **Deirdre O'Donohue,** Former *USA Today* book reviewer, for her insights on this publication.

- **Joni Wilson,** Perhaps the finest proofreader we have dealt with.

- **Gary Milgrom,** Atlantapixel.com, for the cover design.

> *Dedicated to all those who look at space for what it is and dream of what it can be.*
>
> *Who see the industry as a place to do business, bring the world closer together, better the planet, or explore the galaxy.*
>
> *Who don't just dream, but also look at the space industry and see a career.*

FOREWORD

THE FUTURE AHEAD: YOUR PATHWAY TO TOMORROW

Embarking on a career in space is a challenging endeavor, one that can surely become an adventure of a lifetime. For me, personally, my experience as an astronaut drew upon skills that I had honed throughout high school, during undergraduate work at West Point, at Air Force fighter pilot school, and then at the Massachusetts Institute of Technology (MIT). That's where I earned my Doctorate in Astronautics. My MIT thesis was on Manned Orbital Rendezvous.

But first let me talk about tenacity.

My early aim of becoming an astronaut was short-circuited. I had my NASA application first turned down because I wasn't a test pilot. But due to my strong-willed resolve to seek out a career as an astronaut, I applied again. This time, my jet fighter pilot know-how and NASA's budding interest in mastering the art of space rendezvous influenced them to accept me. And, in October 1963, I became a member of the third group of NASA-chosen astronauts. By the way, I was the first astronaut selected with a doctorate and became known to my fellow astronauts as "Dr. Rendezvous."

My timing was just right for stepping into the space program. I asked myself how best to apply my experience as a fighter pilot and expertise in guidance and navigation. Back then, joining objects in space was something that was only done by computer analysis or discussed in academic circles through a paper or two. In fact, I could count on the fingers of one hand experts in the field of space rendezvous. I took a hard look at rendezvous methods and boiled them down to simple terms, in essence, a seat-of-the-pants approach.

The merit of my rendezvous ideas gradually gathered adherence. It afforded the pilots—the astronauts—a way to have backup charts, make measurements, and assure that we were contributing to a spacecraft's flight. The essence of my rendezvous techniques was tested during Gemini, then applied to the Apollo lunar landing effort, and is still used today. I am very proud of that contribution—one that gave Neil Armstrong and me the distinctive achievement of becoming the first humans to set foot on the Moon in July 1969.

For those of you just starting on a high-technology career path, I can offer some observations that may prove helpful. They have been valuable to me.

I came up with a philosophy several years ago of trying to go through life with my arms outstretched to cut a wide swath. Gather in as many things as possible into your realm of awareness. You will be surprised at what you encounter and collect.

Don't focus too narrowly. Open up. Change direction. Look at a problem from as many perspectives as enter into your mind. Add to somebody's idea or bring two people together who are working the same problem, but from different points of view. Polish your ideas as much as possible, then try them out on others. Don't be afraid to give away a little bit in order to become a cooperative person. To say you need an open mind is obvious.

During the past years, it has become clear that a young person's scientific and technical career can be fueled by a passion for science, technology, engineering, and math—a combination of disciplines dubbed STEM. But let me add one more ingredient: the arts.

Science, technology, engineering, arts, and math (STEAM) power is the way to go. And through my Buzz Aldrin ShareSpace Foundation I strongly support the belief that by incorporating arts into the STEM equation even greater results will be achieved by people at all stages of their education.

Regarding work skills, the fact that you are reading these words already indicates your ability to research and stay current. You should keep abreast of space projects underway in the private sector, in academic settings, and in the government. Maintaining your knowledge of world space progress is very important.

By the way, there are two other skills that are very critical. Written and verbal communication skills are a must. I've seen many a creative idea, prompted by brilliant deduction, stymied because he or she could not convey to others their thoughts in a coherent or persuasive manner. Furthermore, project into the future and consider how your creative viewpoint might contribute to the betterment of conditions today. Think about how best to take advantage of the microgravity, the vacuum, the three-dimensional freedom, the view from a distance that space offers.

Last, the most powerful tool you can acquire or experience is an ability to give away what you have just learned, to teach someone the basics of what you are attempting to understand.

There is much to do in assuring that humankind moves forward in its space pursuits. For me, I am sharply focusing my energies on reusable first-stage rocketry, the opening up of a space tourism market, and the creation of a sustainable space program. I envision future use of cycling orbits that form a network supporting inner-solar system traffic of cargo, men and women that ply routinely between the Earth and Mars. Beautiful simplicity coupled with a ballet of intricate celestial mechanics are the hallmarks of this approach. Reusable, recyclable space transportation is the key to our future. Fashioning a sustainable space program is paramount to becoming a true, spacefaring civilization.

I encourage you to read through this informative book. You will note that a diversity of potential space careers is available to you, as are the types of industries involved.

Let me close by being a bit blunt. It will take more than rhetoric to assure that a strong and imaginative 21st-century space program becomes reality. We must remain steadfast in our resolve to create new economic opportunity in space, assure the integrity and security of our home planet Earth, expand meaningful American cooperation in space with other nations, establish a permanent foothold on Mars, and move humanity outward into the universe at large.

I'm sure you've heard your parents or others tell you that "the world is yours"—and they are right. But I want to take it even one step further and let you know that "the worlds are yours" as well!

Best wishes for selecting the discipline that suits your interests, and good luck in contributing to the space program in the years ahead.

Dr. Buzz Aldrin
Gemini 12 and *Apollo 11* Astronaut
Satellite Beach, Florida

INTRODUCTION

"One small step for man, one giant leap for mankind"[1]
"In a galaxy, far, far, away"[2]
"Space, the final frontier"[3]

These words have inspired billions of people around the Earth, and the great space race to the Moon in the 1960s enabled many to live out a dream. Today, hundreds of thousands of people from all walks of life and all backgrounds have chosen to work in a space industry that is far larger and more diverse than ever before.

By choosing a career in the space industry, you can be part of today's vision—whether it means bringing the world closer together through communications systems, monitoring and preserving the Earth's climate and resources, or building rockets and satellites to explore the solar system, the galaxy, and the wider universe.

Though many do not realize it, the space industry is much bigger and broader than human space programs, such as the International Space Station, programs to take people to the Moon and Mars, or the rockets that enable private space tourists.

In fact, according to recent statistics, the space and satellite industry generates more than 20 times the revenues that Hollywood generates at the U.S. box office. And when accounting for all the revenues generated by spacecraft distributing or offering information, communications, and entertainment services to consumers and businesses, it is roughly half the size of the global software industry.[4]

The space industry employs an estimated 71,500 aerospace engineers with a median salary of $105,450;[5] nearly 3,000 atmospheric and space scientists[6] in the government alone; and is part of an Aerospace Product & Parts Manufacturing (NAICS 336 400) sector that employs more than 502,000. This does not even include the tens of thousands of people who are classified as working in communications and other fields. According to the "U.S. Space Industry Deep Dive" produced by the U.S. Department of Commerce, the 611 space-dependent respondents to their survey stated total employment of nearly 350,000 people.

Space is a place for jobs, many of them high-paying—one of which could be a career for you.

WHAT WILL THIS BOOK DO FOR ME?

Whether you are a student in high school, at the university level, employed in the space industry, or hoping to find a new position within it, *Space Careers* can help you.

It is designed to give you the resources you need and provide you with valuable insights, so that you can have a better understanding of the industry and identify the opportunities within it.

Among the valuable information this book will impart is:

- An understanding of the role and activities of industry, government, military, and academia.
- The different types of positions/careers available.
- Financing your education: scholarships and fellowships.
- How to increase employment prospects.
- Universities that specialize in space.

- Where to find information on open positions.
- Why, how, and where to network.
- Words of wisdom on résumés and interviewing.

And for those hoping to explore space on a personal level, this book gives details on becoming a professional astronaut.

Along the way, you'll get a range of resources and links including *contact information and links to leading companies and organizations.*

WHAT IS THE SPACE INDUSTRY?

The space industry is as diverse as any that exists in today's economy. Although human spaceflight endeavors, such as space tourism or dreams of Mars exploration, get the most attention, people working within the space and satellite industry are involved in everything from engineering and science to manufacturing, farming, geology, and meteorology to sales, marketing, policy, and international relations.

The space industry can actually be thought of as a combination of other industries—communications, electronics, information technology, computers and software, environmental monitoring, manufacturing, medical and biotechnology research, etc. In fact, many of the people who are actually involved in or who use the industry in their work, consider themselves part of other industries. Ask a medical researcher what they are involved in and chances are they will say that they are seeking a cure for Alzheimer's or cancer, not someone involved with evaluating pure crystals manufactured in the microgravity of space.

An overview of the activities that encompass the space industry is presented in Chapter 2. Take notice…many of the activities in the space industry actually take place on the ground and not all are science or engineering related. There are lots of jobs.

WHAT TYPES OF JOBS ARE THERE?
...For Engineers, Scientists, and Technologists

People working in the sector have diverse backgrounds that are as varied as the industry itself. Common degrees for engineers and technical managers might be aerospace engineering, mechanical engineering, electrical engineering, chemical engineering, materials engineering, and systems engineering. Degrees in computer science and programming and information technology are always in demand. The tasks they could be working on relate to structural testing, aerodynamics, rocket propulsion, avionics, guidance navigation and control, and orbital mechanics. They could be developing and testing breadboards or electronic devices or programming software to track and monitor the performance of spacecraft. Other staff could be focused on environmental and human factors issues, resolving network interference, or monitoring space debris. Scientists could be monitoring the planet and weather patterns, using the results from microgravity experiments to identify new biotech compounds, or studying the universe.

WHAT TYPE OF ENGINEERING OR SCIENCE BACKGROUND SHOULD I PURSUE?

Aerospace Engineering	Astronomy	Astrophysics
Chemical Engineering	Communications	Computer Science
Data Analysis	Electrical Engineering	Fluid Mechanics
Human Factors	Information Technology	Materials Engineering
Mechanical Engineering	Meteorology	Optics & Electro Optics
Physics	Software	Systems Engineering

WHAT TYPES OF JOBS ARE THERE?
...For Architects, Archaeologists, Geologists, Farmers, and More!

Professionals in a variety of fields use products derived from the space industry. Architects and civil planners use satellite data and digital maps to locate, evaluate, and understand construction sites. Geologists use satellite data to find possible mineral deposits. Archaeologists have begun using space imagery to locate sites located under hundreds of feet of sand or on the ocean bottom.

Farmers are increasingly relying on remotely sensed data to learn about the health of their crops and guide them to areas that need fertilizer or water. They may also use Global Positioning System satellites to automate their tractors and harvesters.

CAN I FIND SOMETHING WITHOUT A TECHNICAL DEGREE?

Though they don't get the publicity, a large number of the people who work in the space industry do not have technical backgrounds, but they apply their skills to do what many know as a highly technical industry.

Careers exist for people with skills in:

Business Development	Sales and Marketing	Accounting
Technical Writing	Human Resources	Policy
Employee Relations	Conference Management	Law
Graphic Design	Administration	Contracting
International Relations	Public Relations	Finance/Investing
Journalism	Economics	Manufacturing

ARE THERE "GREEN" OPPORTUNITIES?

There is no technology responsible for bringing the world closer together than the space and satellite industry. Satellite data is enabling professionals to monitor weather patterns, plot the migration of fish and animals, track the outbreak of diseases, and determine the health and well-being of our planet.

WHAT IF I DON'T LIVE NEAR A NASA FACILITY?

Although there might be a higher concentration of companies involved with space in some parts of the United States, particularly near NASA and military research facilities, companies and organizations involved with space and telecommunications can be found throughout North America and the world. A review of the organizations listed in Appendix B shows a diversity of firms located throughout the United States and Canada

DREAMING THE FUTURE— WHAT ARE THE OPPORTUNITIES?

Whether initiatives by NASA tackling a post-Shuttle environment, entrepreneurial ventures funded by deep-pocket investors to offer expanded tourism activities, or an ever-more integrated global world that relies on satellites for communications, information, environmental monitoring, and entertainment…this is an exciting time. New paths to the future are being defined and more will undoubtedly emerge. During the past 25 years, space assets have revolutionized communications and video and data services and provided us with a better understanding of our planet and our environment. Within the next 25 years, many within the industry believe that we will:

- Land humans on Mars.
- Perform research on orbiting space platforms with revolutionary results.
- Provide broadband Internet access to the entire planet, even in remote areas,
- Monitor the planet and be able to predict weather patterns with greater efficacy,
- Expand spaceflight opportunities to the average citizen,
- Harness the Sun's energy with solar power stations.
- Identify, mitigate, and respond to potential disasters, such as earthquakes or volcano eruptions.

As the industry evolves throughout time, the industry can grow in directions not dreamed of today.

You can be a part of that growth.

---

1 Neil Armstrong's first words upon setting foot on the Moon.

2 Quote from Star Wars © and ™ Lucasfilm, Ltd.

3 Star Trek and related elements © and ™ Paramount Pictures Corporation.

4 Gartner estimate: size of the worldwide software industry in 2013 was US$407.3 billion.

5 Bureau of Labor Statistics, 2014.

6 Department of Labor, 2014.

WHAT IS THE SPACE INDUSTRY?

In this chapter:

The space industry is literally comprised of hundreds of different activities. This brief chapter will provide you with a list to expose you to the diversity.

"But for pennies on the dollar, the space program has fueled jobs and entire industries. For pennies on the dollar, the space program has improved our lives, advanced our society, strengthened our economy, and inspired generations of Americans…

"The space race inspired a generation of scientists and innovators, including, I'm sure, many of you. It's contributed to immeasurable technological advances that have improved our health and well-being, from satellite navigation to water purification, from aerospace manufacturing to medical imaging."

U.S. President Barack Obama

WHAT OR WHERE IS SPACE?

There is no agreed-to legal definition of where space begins. Different groups have their own definitions about where the Earth's atmosphere ends and space begins. Scientists have classified space as beginning approximately 200–300 nautical miles above the Earth's surface. Aeronautical engineers generally use 54 nautical miles, because aerodynamic forces are negligible above this height. The U.S. Air Force defines space as heights above 44 nautical miles.

In conventional and customary law, the major space powers generally accept "the lowest altitude attained by orbiting space vehicles" as the threshold of space. This point, the lowest at which a satellite can maintain a stable orbit, is 90 nautical miles. To maintain this altitude, a satellite must have a minimum velocity of 17,500 miles per hour parallel to the surface of the Earth.

Ninety miles up, the temperature is as low as -450F or 3K; gravity is less than 1/1000 of that which would be felt on Earth; and radiation is much higher and more damaging than that on Earth.

But this harsh environment offers a unique perspective on the Earth below. Like looking off the top of a tall building or a mountain and gazing across the land below, the vantage point of space offers an opportunity to scan the Earth's surface, thereby providing a platform for remote sensing, weather monitoring, intelligence gathering, and communications. And from space, satellites reach most of the world's population, every day, in one way or another.

THE SPACE INDUSTRY ENCOMPASSES...

Infrastructure

Spacecraft Manufacturing (Construction of the satellites)

Communications Satellites	Remote-Sensing Satellites
Planetary Exploration Satellites	Weather Satellites
Spacecraft for Military Application Satellites	R&D Technology

Launch Vehicles (Rockets used to place payloads in orbit)

Expendable Launch Vehicles	Reusable Launch Vehicles

Ground Equipment (The equipment on Earth that is used to receive and/or transmit data to and from spacecraft)

Ground Stations	Command and Control
Antennas	Teleport Facilities
High Capacity Data Storage	Telemetry Systems
Receiving & Transmission Equipment	

Ground Operations (Facility design, development, and use; monitoring and controlling spacecraft or launch vehicles)

Launch Vehicle Operations	Spaceports
Spacecraft Operations	Schedule and Planning
Software and Systems	Component Test Facilities
Health Monitoring and Operations Planning Software	

Human Space Activities (Activities related to the human exploration of space and effects of long- and short-duration spaceflight on the human condition)

International Space Station	Human Flight Vehicles
Medical, Physiological, and Psychological Research	

Satellite Services

Information, Communications, and Entertainment
(Using spacecraft to relay data from one part of Earth to another)

- Video Program Distribution
- Live News and Sports Transmission
- Mobile and Wireless Communications
- International Telephony
- VSAT and Private Networks
- Direct-to-Consumer Video and Radio
- Broadband Internet Access
- Telemedicine and Tele-Education

Global Positioning System Services (The use of satellite networks provides accurate positioning data anywhere on Earth)

- Enhanced Air Traffic Control
- Directional Services for Automobiles
- Logistics: Maritime Fleet Management
- Logistics: Land Vehicle Fleet Management
- Logistics: Cargo Tracking
- Mapping of Cities and Roads
- Navigation for Boaters and Hikers
- Improved Search and Rescue

Remote Sensing (The monitoring of Earth using space-based sensors)

- Weather Prediction and Forecasting
- Monitoring of the Earth's Environment
- Searching for Natural Resources
- Oceanographic Forecasting
- Analysis of Soil and Land Conditions for Farming
- Use of Digital Terrain Maps
- National Security Intelligence Gathering
- Land Development and Planning
- Change Pattern Recognition

Humanitarian Operations

- Disaster and Crisis Prevention and Management
- Post-Crisis Communications and Logistics

Scientific Research

Microgravity (Use of the special environmental conditions in space—such as low temperature and low gravity—to develop materials or products)
- Production of New or Improved Materials
- Enhanced Crystals for Biomedical Research
- Biomedical Drug Development

Space Science (The study of the universe, including stars, planets, interstellar materials, and the effect of the space environment on the Earth)
- Astrophysics and Astronomy   Astrodynamics
- Cosmology   Astrobiology
- Search for Extraterrestrial Intelligence (SETI)

Technology Research and Development (A number of technologies are used in various aspects of the industry)
- Lasers and Optics   Power Systems
- Propulsion Systems   Thermal Control
- Composite Materials   Robotics
- High-Temperature Materials   Control Systems

Support Activities

- Administrative Support   Technical Support
- Legal and Licensing   Financial Services
- Media and Publishing   Public & Media Relations
- Marketing and Sales
- Satellite, Launch Vehicle, and In-Orbit Insurance

Future Space Activities

- Tourism and Space Adventures   Permanent Lunar Bases
- Human Missions to Mars   Mining of Asteroids
- Manufacturing in Orbital Facilities Solar Power Stations
- Orbital Solar Power Generation Stations Toxic Waste Disposal
- Satellite Servicing and Repair

WORKING IN THE SPACE INDUSTRY

Biography & Advice

Name	Debra Facktor Lepore
Organization	Ball Aerospace & Technologies
Job Title	Vice President/GM, Strategic Operations
Location	Arlington, Virginia
Link	www.ballaerospace.com

Responsibilities

I am the vice president and general manager of Strategic Operations for Ball Aerospace. My organization consists of three divisions: Washington Operations, Communications, and Strategic Developments. I'm responsible for increasing Ball Aerospace's presence in the market and facilitating collaboration across our company, and serve as the company's senior representative in the Washington, DC, area.

Degrees/School

B.S.E. and M.S.E., aerospace engineering, University of Michigan
International Space University, summer session program (space policy & law)

Career Path

I began work during the Cold War as an aerospace engineer at ANSER, a think tank in the Washington, DC area. At ANSER, I worked on advanced launch vehicles, became an expert on Russian rocket engines, and then served as chief of Moscow Operations during the very early days of establishing cooperation with Russia and Ukraine on space activities. This led me to the entrepreneurial part of my career, where I worked at Kistler Aerospace Corporation to develop the privately funded K-1 reusable launch vehicle, and then as president of AirLaunch LLC, developing a small rocket to launch out of the back of a C-17 cargo aircraft. After the start-ups, I did an academic sabbatical at Stevens Institute of Engineering in systems engineering, and then joined Ball Aerospace at the beginning of 2013.

Why Space?

I chose space because I wanted to work on things that had never been done before. I grew up outside of Detroit, Michigan, surrounded by the automotive industry. Apparently this influenced me, as I ended up working on rocket engines and launch vehicles—a transportation industry of a different kind!

Words of Wisdom

I have benefited from advice of many mentors over the years and learned from my own experiences. To this day, I use my own guiding principle of "doing things that have never been done before" to make career or life decisions. I firmly believe in "passing it on"—in mentoring, sharing advice, helping others, and creating a community of collaboration.

HISTORY

In this chapter:

A brief history of space from the first science-fiction ideas, the first rocket launches landing on the Moon, to missions for the space industry of tomorrow. Only by understanding the past, can we understand the present and the future.

It is difficult to say what is impossible,
For the dream of yesterday is the hope of today
And the reality of tomorrow

—Robert H. Goddard
Father of American rocketry

SCI-FI HISTORY IN THE MAKING

To boldly go where no one has gone before...is a saying deeply rooted in the popular movie and television presentations of *Star Trek*.

But in truth, that premise of space exploration has been alive and well for centuries, from the earliest beginnings of science fiction writing to the theater screens of today. The use of imagination as propulsion can transport a person outward to the Moon or at warp speed to faraway stars and their companion planets.

Take, for instance, Cyrano de Bergerac, who in the early 1600s wrote a story making use of rocket propulsion to commute to the Moon. More than two hundred years later, writer Edward Everett Hale detailed in the *Atlantic Monthly* what is thought to be the first fictional account of a space station. In 1869 and 1870 issues of the magazine, Hale concocted a tale of a large brick satellite, housing 37 adventurers.

Cruising at a cosmic altitude high above Earth, Hale's whimsical postulations had the crew of the brick satellite aiding navigating seaman below. To communicate with sailors, the brick moon's residents jumped up and down on the exterior of the satellite in Morse code fashion: long bounds for dashes, short leaps for dots!

In similar manner, but based on more solid technical footing, were the writings of Jules Verne. In his classic 1865 novel, *From the Earth to the Moon,* he wrote of a bullet-shaped space ship resembling, in many ways, the launch vehicles of today. Verne painted a picture of space travel featuring conditions commonly encountered by 20th-century human explorers. His notion of rocket propulsion, however, was to utilize a huge cannon to fire a passenger-riding projectile to the Moon.

Following on the heels of Verne, was the H. G. Wells 1897 account that detailed a Martian invasion of Earth—the *Independence Day* movie of its time—*The War of the Worlds*. The fanciful tales of Verne and Wells were soon not so fanciful. The technology of flight, first by aircraft and then by rockets, jumped from fictional verbiage to high-velocity hardware.

It was science fiction that helped seed the imaginings of many a "real" rocketeer.

PIONEERING IMAGINEERS

Like the harnessing of the atom, the erection of the Grand Coulee dam in Washington state or the construction of the Panama Canal, spaceflight symbolizes technological achievement in the 20th century. Russian scientist and father of astronautics Konstantin Tsiolkovsky; German scientist Hermann Oberth; America's Robert Goddard; and consummate space visionary Wernher von Braun, to name but a few, shaped the foundation of thought on space. Each plotted out a master plan for utilizing space. Each developed a blueprint for opening the frontier of space, predicated not on fanciful fiction but on the mathematical and scientific knowledge of the day. These individuals were part of a vanguard of visionaries who turned dream machines into reality.

Called the father of American rocketry, Goddard was first inspired by Jules Verne's *From the Earth to the Moon*, as well as the writings of H.G. Wells. He earned his science degree from Worcester Polytechnic Institute in Massachusetts and, as a young engineer, received his first patent for a "rocket apparatus" in 1914. Shortly thereafter, as a part-time physics professor at Clark University, he crafted his first rockets. It was in this period that Goddard wrote his seminal paper submitted to the Smithsonian Institution and published in 1919: *A Method of Reaching Extreme Altitudes*.

It was Goddard, at a time when Oberth and Tsiolkovsky theorized space futures, who began putting metal into the sky by the late 1920s.
His inventions were modest in the beginning. The world's first liftoff of a liquid-fueled rocket, in fact, took place from the snow-

covered Massachusetts farm of Goddard's Aunt Effie. That rocket flight on March 16, 1926, lasted a little more than two seconds, shooting to an altitude of 184 feet. A few years later, seeking a site with good weather for year-round testing and distant from populated areas, Goddard continued his pioneering work in Roswell, New Mexico, where he remained until 1941. From fuel pumps to guidance and control gyroscopes, Goddard pursued many innovations that would later become mainstay technology for all large rockets.

Robert Goddard's impressive accomplishments, along with the growing body of work by Tsiolkovsky and Oberth, inspired many others around the globe. Among them was Wernher von Braun.

At the close of World War II, the U.S. Army seized the top engineers of Germany's rocket effort, including von Braun. He and his engineering team (along with some captured V-2 rockets) were brought to the United States and stationed at the Army's White Sands Proving Grounds in New Mexico. It was from this talent base that America's space program was formed.

To most Americans in the late 1940s and early 1950s, space travel was relegated to the backs of cereal boxes and the latest installment of *Flash Gordon* in the Sunday newspaper. But von Braun sought to challenge people's incredulity by detailing a scientifically accurate, step-by-step approach to space exploration in the pages of popular magazines.

Keen on technical accuracy, von Braun stressed that space travel did not require huge leaps in new technology. Wheel-shaped space stations, an expedition to the planet Mars, even the hauling into Earth orbit the necessary fuel and hardware via a "space ferry" were envisioned by von Braun and explained in matter-of-fact detail as eminently possible.

Part politician, part salesman, full-time rocketeer, von Braun began to captivate millions with his space blueprint.

In early October 1957, people found space travel on their front doorstep. Newspaper headlines screamed that the Soviet Union had hurled *Sputnik 1*, the first artificial satellite, into space. The Space Age had arrived.

BUILDING FROM THE GROUND UP

Sputnik 1's launch on October 4, 1957, proved to be a propaganda coup for the Soviet Union. Even more striking was the orbiting of *Sputnik 2* just four months later. It carried the first living organism—a dog named Laika—into space.

Following the Soviet Union's one-two space punch came America's response. Sitting atop its booster on December 6, 1957, at a Cape Canaveral, Florida, launch site, was the tiny Vanguard satellite. It was all over in one second. On live television, the satellite fell to the ground as part of flaming booster wreckage, later to be found still beeping amid the rubble.

"American Sputnik goes Kaputnik!" complained more than one newspaper headline after the failure. American pride and prestige went up in flames with the satellite.

Vanguard's failure forced President Dwight Eisenhower to order a U.S. Army team to loft a satellite into orbit within 90 days. That team was headed by Wernher von Braun.

The U.S. *Explorer 1* satellite rocketed into orbit on January 31, 1958. At just 30 pounds, the U.S. Explorer satellite weighed just 1/36th the weight of the more massive *Sputnik 2*. In those early, heady days of U.S. and Soviet one-upmanship, bigger meant better, never mind the scientific utility of a satellite.

For many Americans, those first Soviet satellite successes signaled something akin to a technological Pearl Harbor in space. With the lofting of America's *Explorer 1*, a two-nation "space race" was on.

In early 1958, the U.S. Congress passed the National Aeronautics and Space Act, signed into law on July 29 by President Eisenhower. America's commitment to space was born out of the government-industry partnerships the nation had made for aeronautical research. The National Advisory Committee for Aeronautics (NACA) was transformed into the National Aeronautics and Space Administration (NASA). At the same time, a largely classified military space program began to grow in the Pentagon.

Almost one year to the day after *Sputnik 1* began circling Earth, NASA officially started to orchestrate the nation's civilian space agenda. By the end of 1960, NASA had some 19,000 employees in its ranks. As its partnerships with industry and academia grew, so too did plans for a stable of launch vehicles and various types of application satellites and scientific probes.

Experimental Earth remote sensing, weather, navigation, and communications satellites were in orbit by the early 1960s. In the communications arena, NASA's leadership spawned the first operational telecommunications satellite of its type, *Telstar 1*, built by AT&T's Bell Laboratories. Primitive compared to the communications satellites now in use, *Telstar 1* relayed up to 60 telephone calls or a single television channel simultaneously. A few months after *Telstar 1* was launched in July 1962, The Radio Corporation of America (RCA) began operating its *Relay 1* communications satellite. Television networks, also in their infancy in many ways, boasted of programs that were "Live Via Satellite."

From the vantage point of space, satellites afforded new ways to monitor crops; watch for dangerous weather conditions; transmit voice, data, and images around the globe; as well as maintain a vigil for trouble spots that might jeopardize national interests.
But early in the 1960s, it was the combination of politics and romance of the cosmos that supplied the U.S. space program with its most difficult challenges.

THE HUMAN TOUCH

Standing before Congress on May 25, 1961, President John F. Kennedy set America on a course to the Moon.

> *I believe that this nation should commit itself to achieving the goal, before this decade is out, of landing a man on the moon and returning him safely to the earth. No single space project in this period will be more impressive to mankind, or more important for the long-range exploration of space; and none will be so difficult or expensive to accomplish.*[1]

That bold decision was made a month after the Soviet Union's Yuri Gagarin had become the first human to orbit the Earth. Moreover, Kennedy's commitment came just 20 days after a U.S. astronaut had flown a 15-minute "suborbital" flight of a Mercury space capsule. That test shot, a quick, albeit highly televised mission, set in motion America's human spaceflight program that remains active today.

Kennedy's declaration about putting a man on the Moon had provided, in a very real way, a finish line for the "space race" between two superpowers.

There was no question that reaching for the Moon's terra incognita would be daunting. Kennedy himself addressed that fact in September 1962, noting before a 40,000-person gathering at Rice University in Houston, Texas:

> *We shall send to the moon, more than 240,000 miles from the control station in Houston, a giant rocket more than 300 feet tall, the length of this football field, made of new metal alloys, some of which have not yet been invented, capable of standing heat and stresses several times more than have ever been experienced, fitted together with a precision better than the finest watch, carrying all the*

---

[1] http://www.nasa.gov/vision/space/features/jfk_speech_text.html

equipment needed for propulsion, guidance, control, communications, food and survival, on an untried mission, to an unknown celestial body.[2]

Apollo became a work in progress. To reach for the Moon demanded the harnessing of pilot skills and hardware through the Mercury and Gemini space missions. From single-seater flights of Mercury astronauts to the two-person Gemini spacecraft, these piloted space missions around the Earth would provide the nation the necessary wherewithal to reach outward a quarter-of-a-million miles.

But moving from rhetoric to real rocketry meant calling upon government, industry, and university skills. The Apollo effort would consist of more than 20,000 companies employing almost 400,000 people throughout the country.

On July 20, 1969, Earth's collective heartbeat sped up, then the world experienced a heart-stopping moment. A strange shadow fell across the Moon's cratered, grayish landscape. Gliding above a stark vista, billions of years old, an oddly shaped craft hovered in mid-vacuum, its landing legs outstretched. *Apollo 11*'s lunar lander, the *Eagle*, settled down in a place called the Sea of Tranquility. The goal set by President Kennedy, fewer than nine years earlier, had been met.

U.S. astronauts Neil Armstrong and Buzz Aldrin became the first human visitors to another world, as fellow *Apollo 11* astronaut Michael Collins orbited the Moon in an Apollo command module.

As the two moonwalkers explored the lunar surface, history was written in a place Aldrin tagged as "magnificent desolation."

Starting in July 1969 and continuing until December 1972, six expeditionary crews visited the Moon, allowing 12 men from Earth, and a nation, to reach beyond their grasp.

---

[2] http://er.jsc.nasa.gov/seh/ricetalk.htm

AFTER APOLLO

While placing humans on a distant world was the vision of generations, the dream was short-lived. The efforts of 400,000 government workers and hundreds of aerospace contractors and suppliers were left in the lunar dust when *Apollo 17* astronauts departed the Moon in December 1972.

Financial belt tightening by the government led to the cancellation of *Apollos 18, 19,* and *20.* Within a decade, the space agency's budget fell from more than $20 billion in 1964 to $6 billion. With the decline in NASA's funding, visionary schemes of large space stations, bases on the Moon, and sending human expeditions to Mars faltered. Layoffs swept through the industry as the Apollo lunar landing program ended.

During the budget problems of the 1970s, NASA continued its mission by focusing on robotic planetary explorers and using leftover Apollo space hardware.

Among the many automated missions that NASA pursued during this time were Pioneer, Voyager, and the Viking mission to Mars, each of which proved a major success by relaying to Earth valuable data on our solar system and our planetary neighbors.

NASA also initiated two other major programs in this period. Skylab, America's first space station, was crafted by modifying a huge Saturn V upper-stage left over from the Apollo program, and the Apollo-Soyuz Test Project, which led to the first docking in space between a Russian and U.S. spacecraft.

The Skylab space station was lofted into orbit in May 1973. Once in space, Apollo spacecraft were launched to the Earth-circling complex. From May 1973 into November of that year, three separate Apollo spacecraft, each carrying a three-person crew, were lobbed to the Skylab outpost. Years later, abandoned, it re-entered the Earth's atmosphere.

The Apollo-Soyuz Test Project was also designed from ex-Apollo hardware and it signaled the end of the "space race" between the Soviet Union and the United States. High above Earth, a two-person cosmonaut crew linked their Soyuz spacecraft with the three-seater Apollo on July 17, 1975. The docking in orbit was enabled by specially designed hardware, a forerunner of the equipment now in use to couple spacecraft to the *International Space Station*. For the Apollo-Soyuz linkup in Earth orbit, it was handshakes in space and performing joint scientific experiments—all part of the high-altitude détente that took place during two days. That cooperation lapsed for two decades before renewal.

WINGING A WAY TO ORBIT

From 1975 until 1981, the United States astronaut corps was essentially grounded. Technical snags, budgetary squeezes, and a largely disinterested Congress combined to stretch out the development of the U.S. Space Shuttle.

The $10 billion investment in the Space Shuttle program resulted in an initial fleet of orbiters: *Enterprise* (used for air drop tests only), *Columbia, Discovery, Atlantis, Endeavour,* and *Challenger*.

As billed in the 1970s, the Space Shuttle program would be used to ferry materials to and from a space station; resupply, repair, recover, and deploy satellites; as well as act as a winged laboratory in space. The first flight in 1981 proved successful, but the program proved far costlier than NASA and other experts predicted.

Then, 25 Shuttle flights later, the *Challenger* orbiter and its seven crew members were lost en route to orbit. On January 28, 1986, just 73 seconds into flight, a leak in the joint of one of the two solid rocket propellant motors led to the destruction of *Challenger* and the astronauts. Following more than two years of remaking the Shuttle program, *Discovery* winged its way into space on September 29, 1988. The mission paved the way for the dozens of Shuttle launches that followed.

One outcome from the *Challenger* disaster was the rebirth of a private expendable rocket fleet. With the Space Shuttle launching commercial and government payloads, the production and launch of Delta, Atlas, Titan and other expendable launch vehicles diminished in the early 1980s. With the Shuttle fleet grounded for those two years, payloads stacked up on Earth. This helped the commercial launch vehicle industry to establish itself as the primary means for placing payloads into space.

Sadly, during the Space Shuttle program that operated from 1981 into 2011, the loss of *Challenger* was followed in 2003 by the catastrophic destruction of the *Columbia* Space Shuttle orbiter and its seven-person crew. After a 15-day mission in early 2003, that space plane faced fierce heat due to damage of its leading edge reentry tile system as it plowed through Earth's atmosphere. *Columbia* broke apart and fell across eastern Texas and the western Louisiana landscape, with all lives onboard lost.

In 2004, U.S. President George W. Bush announced that the Space Shuttles would be retired. The final Space Shuttle launch was that of *Atlantis* on July 8, 2011, bringing the Space Shuttle program to a close when that orbiter touched down at Kennedy Space Center on July 21, 2011. In total, 135 Space Shuttle flights were attained.

During that time, NASA's fleet of Space Shuttle orbiters traveled to Earth orbit, deployed and repaired satellites, carried out invaluable experiments in microgravity, and successfully delivered key components and crews needed to build and maintain the *International Space Station.*

The three remaining orbiters from the program—*Discovery*, *Atlantis*, and *Endeavour*, and the prototype shuttle, *Enterprise*—are now housed in various museums throughout the country.

With the Space Shuttle effort now retired, NASA has turned its attention to the next phase of human space exploration—designing and building the spacecraft needed to send humans deeper into the solar system, working toward a goal of putting people on Mars.

The space agency is now focused on the Orion Multi-Purpose Crew Vehicle and the Space Launch System, an advanced heavy-lift booster designed for human exploration beyond Earth's orbit.

In addition, NASA partnered with private companies, such as Space Exploration Technologies Corporation (or SpaceX) and Orbital Sciences, to provide cargo flights to the *International Space Station*. More recently, NASA selected SpaceX and Boeing to supply human-carrying spacecraft that would propel crews to the *ISS*.

A WATCHFUL EYE—CLASSIFIED

Throughout it all, from the years before the launch of *Sputnik* to the current day, while NASA and civil space activities have provided a public focus on space, the U.S. military and intelligence communications have relied on satellites for communications, monitoring for missile launches, rocket development, sensor development, etc.

Without doubt, many important innovations have come from these efforts—many of them classified.

For its part, the United States Air Force provides air, space, and cyber capabilities for use by the combatant commanders. Under its leadership, the U.S. Air Force provides "Spacelift" operations at east coast and west coast launch bases, provides services, facilities and range safety control for the conduct of DoD, NASA, and commercial launches.

Through the command and control of all DoD satellites, satellite operators provide "force-multiplying effects" —that is, continuous global coverage, low vulnerability, and autonomous operations. Satellites provide essential secure communications, weather and navigational data for ground, air and fleet operations, and threat warning.

For example, the U.S. military space operators involve Space-Based Infrared System and Defense Support Program satellites that monitor ballistic missile launches around the world to guard against a surprise missile attack on North America. Additionally, space surveillance radars provide vital information on the location of satellites and space debris.

In recent years, the threat of cyberspace attacks has drawn added attention. The Air Force carries out its core missions through air, space, and cyberspace. Through cyberspace operations, the Air Force is dedicated to finding and using the best tools, skills, and capabilities to ensure the ability to fly, fight, and win in air, space, and cyberspace.

Additionally, the eyes and ears of the United States in critical places where no human can reach—be it over the most rugged terrain or through the most hostile territory—is an essential role of the National Reconnaissance Office (NRO). The NRO is the U.S. government agency in charge of designing, building, launching, and maintaining America's intelligence satellites. NRO creates cutting-edge innovations in satellite technology, contracts with the most cost-efficient industrial suppliers, carries out rigorous launch campaigns, and provides the high-quality products to its customers.

From NRO's inception in 1961 to its declassification to the public in 1992, this organization has worked to provide reconnaissance support to the intelligence community and the Department of Defense. NRO's vision tells the story, albeit secret: Vigilance from Above.

TOWARD A PRIVATE EYE ON SPACE

The seeds for commercial space endeavors were planted in the 1960s. But it is only in the past two decades that many of the early applications have emerged to become economically significant, generating billions in revenues.

The 1960s saw satellite communications essentially begin as an intergovernmental activity; but it wasn't until the 1990s and the emergence of the Internet and the digital era that a privatized satcom services market began to expand significantly. Today this market generates more than $100 billion annually providing information, communications, and entertainment services around the globe. Likewise, commercial services providing imagery from space, Earth monitoring, and global positioning and navigation— all play an increasing role in commerce. Space is emerging as a place for business and commerce, not just exploration. That said, private exploration initiatives are on the rise as well, and many find the opportunities truly exciting.

Understanding History Puts You One Step Closer to Understanding the Present

History reminds us that the quest to push back frontiers on Earth begins with exploration and discovery, followed by settlement and economic development.

Recall the epic journey of Lewis and Clark, sparked by the acquisition of new land through the Louisiana Purchase. Remember the investment made a generation later for what was then termed the "frozen wasteland" called Alaska. Since the earliest times, expansion into new regions is almost always met by skepticism. The risk of a return on investment is high, with patience and fortitude required to win a payoff.

Today, space is paying off. New goods and services for individuals and businesses on Earth result from space commerce. Tapping the unique vantage point of space has led to a wide array of telecommunications services, to prospecting for new energy sources, and to better management of agricultural resources. The vacuum and microgravity conditions found in Earth orbit might lead to improved manufacturing processes or techniques to produce superior electronic components and life-saving drugs.

The use of space for economic expansion is not only being explored by U.S. interests but also by countries around the world. More than 30 nations are actively pursuing space-related opportunities. Japan, France, Germany, Russia, China, Canada, Brazil, Israel, Australia, for example, have recognized the tremendous market potential for commercial space operations. Today, space is no longer just the province of superpowers—it's a key component of the global marketplace.

WORKING IN THE SPACE INDUSTRY

Biography & Advice

Name   Dan Durda
Organization   Southwest Research Institute
Job Title   Principal Scientist
Location   Boulder, Colorado
Link   http://www.boulder.swri.edu/~durda/

Responsibilities

As the Principal Investigator for a number of NASA- (and occasionally NSF-) funded research grants I formulate the research project goals and objectives, manage the conduct of the project (which for me also usually includes working with several Co-Investigators), and lead the writing of resulting publications and conference abstracts.

Degrees/School

B.S. Astronomy, University of Michigan
M.S. Astronomy, University of Florida
Ph.D. Astronomy, University of Florida

Career Path

I decided early on to take an academic path in astronomical research. I worked directly through undergraduate and graduate school, proceeding to several years of post-doctoral work before being hired at Southwest Research Institute where I have worked since 1998.

Why Space?

I was always, from my very earliest childhood memories, interested in science in general, and in space/astronomical topics specifically. By early high school I had already firmly decided on an academic path toward a PhD in Astronomy. During my graduate studies I came in more direct contact with the Space Shuttle program and many astronauts and decided that my skills and interests might be well-matched to working as an astronaut as well. I interviewed as a finalist for the NASA 2004 astronaut class and today am one of three suborbital payload specialists at the company I work for.

Words of Wisdom

Be tenacious and creative. Hone your "people" and communication skills—be a good team member and value the inputs and advice from those you work with. If you don't already, learn to like to write proposals to raise the funds to do the work you want to do.

INSIDE THE SPACE ECONOMY

In this chapter:

As you already may have grasped, the business of space is a broad, diverse industry that offers numerous opportunities. Finding your focus can be a challenge, but starting with your passion is a good first step. To help you begin this journey, this chapter is designed to give you a better understanding of what four estates constitute space: civil government, military, commercial, and academia.

---

* * *

From the birth of the Space Age in the late 1950s through the mid-1980s, space was predominantly a government-driven enterprise. Even today, the U.S. government remains the largest single customer and client for space hardware, software, and services. It remains a driving force behind many efforts, especially those related to human spaceflight endeavors where the resources committed by NASA greatly exceed that of any other organization. U.S. military activities related to satellites for communications, launch, operations, and monitoring the planet maintain a budget that exceeds that of NASA.

The opening of satellite communications to private, non-governmental, and inter-governmental organizations in the 1980s, combined with the opening of the commercial rocket launch business in the aftermath of the Space Shuttle *Challenger* accident in 1986, began a transformation of the sector and opened the commercial sector to pursuing more ventures than just supporting government efforts. By the late 1990s, revenues generated from commercial activities surpassed government expenditures for the first time. Much of this revenue resulted from the use of satellites for information, communications, and entertainment, with the distribution and transmission of video programming driving the sector.

Today, the industry continues to expand and attract interest. It is vital to national security as well as disaster mitigation and response; critical to weather monitoring; a fundamental part of science and technological leadership; a source of national pride, and a vital element to provide information, communications, and entertainment in an increasingly digital and mobile world. The evidence of the integration of space into the global economy is all around us—whenever we access the Internet, while flying on a plane, or looking at the latest weather forecast. Regardless of the career you decide to pursue, this is an exciting time when new economic paths are emerging.

Public companies, private companies, government agencies, military organizations, universities, and research institutions all play a role in the space industry. Understanding the roles and activities of each will enable the job hunter to identify opportunities. Ultimately, your career will find you working for one of these four types of organizations:

1. Civil government space
2. Military space
3. Commercial space
4. Academia

GOVERNMENT: THE SPACE INDUSTRY'S LARGEST CUSTOMER

"No one person, no one company, no one government agency,
has a monopoly on the competence, the missions, or the
requirements for the space program"

U.S. President Lyndon Johnson

* * *

Space remains a vital national interest to the U.S. government for both civil and military activities. The military and intelligence communities continue to integrate space assets and information into their everyday activities. To highlight its importance, speeches by Air Force officials have long stated that the organization is actually an "Air and Space Force".

The government is also the prime mover in a number of major civilian programs, including the International Space Station, the Orion and Commercial Crew vehicles, and a host of smaller science-oriented missions, including rovers visiting the planet Mars. In addition, research performed with the *Hubble Space Telescope* and other space observatories continues to provide amazing data about the universe.

With budgets for civil government, military, and intelligence space activities expected to remain stable for the foreseeable future, they provide a hefty $40 billion annually.

THE CIVIL SPACE SECTOR

The U.S. government is involved in a wide range of non-military activities, from monitoring Earth's weather, to human and robotic exploration of the solar system, to regulating the frequencies that satellite communications operate in.

Although NASA receives the largest budget and is the primary organization for space science and exploration in the United States, other agencies play a significant role from the weather related activities of National Oceanic and Atmospheric Administration (NOAA), the commercial launch safety responsibility of the Federal Aviation Administration, to activities performed by the Department of Commerce, the Federal Communications Commission (FCC), Environmental Protection Agency (EPA), Department of the Interior, and the Federal Emergency Management Agency (FEMA).

With an annual budget of more than $17 billion, NASA is the lead civilian agency for advancing the state-of-the-art in technology and hardware development, the utilization of space data and resources, and science and space exploration.

Federal Agency Space Budgets

Budget Authority in Millions—Real Year Dollars
(Aerospace Report to the President)

Agency	Activity	Budget ($M)
NASA	Science, communications, remote sensing, launch vehicles, human spaceflight	17,898
Dept of Interior	Remote sensing	66
Dept of Commerce (including NOAA)	Remote sensing, weather forecasting, trade promotion	1,444
DoT	Launch regulatory	15
NSF	Research grants	412
DoE	Nuclear / power systems	229
DoD (Unclassified)	Communications, remote sensing, launch vehicles, data analysis, ground operations	27,234

CIVIL SPACE: NASA

While many think of NASA as a well-funded agency, its budget is actually modest compared to other parts of the government. Considering the importance of science, technology, engineering, and math to the U.S. economy, NASA's $17+ billion budget is small compared to the nearly $500 billion discretionary budget for the Department of Defense or the $1.02 trillion budget for the Department of Health and Human Services. In relation to the total U.S. budget, NASA's funding is less than half of one percent of total government outlays.

Major Areas of NASA Interest
NASA's roughly 19,000 employees work on a variety of programs.

- **Science,** including astrophysics, planetary science, Earth science, medical research, and microgravity
- **Human spaceflight,** including the *International Space Station* and new vehicle development
- **Advanced technology development**
- **Transfer of NASA-developed technology** to the overall economy

	FY2015	FY2019*
Earth Science	1.77B	1.89B
Planetary Science	1.28B	1.37B
Astrophysics	607M	933M
James Webb Space Telescope	645M	305M
Heliophysics	669M	676M
Aeronautics	551M	574M
Space Technology	705M	734M
Exploration System Development	2.78B	3.11B
Commercial Spaceflight	848M	172M
Exploration R&D	343M	395M
International Space Station	3.05B	3.82B
Space & Flight Support	855M	783M
Agency Management & Operations	2.78B	2.89B
Facility Construction	446M	390M

* Projected

Who Works at NASA? (courtesy of NASA.gov)

Professional, Engineering and Scientific (60% of positions)

Occupations in this category require knowledge in a specialized field, such as science, math, engineering, law, or accounting (depending on the specific position). These positions generally require a bachelor's degree or higher degree with major study in a specialized field.

Administrative and Management (24% of positions)

Occupations in this category require knowledge of principles, concepts, and practices associated with organizations, administration, or management. While these positions do not require specialized education (except for contracting positions), they do involve the type of skills (analytical, research, writing, judgment) typically gained through a college-level education, or through progressively responsible experience. This group covers positions such as contract specialist, administrative specialist, budget analyst, public affairs, and IT specialist.

Clerical and Administrative Support (7% of positions)

Occupations in this category provide general office or program support duties, such as preparing, receiving, reviewing, and verifying documents; processing transactions; maintaining office records; or locating and compiling data or information from files.

Technical and Medical Support (9% of positions)

Occupations in this category support professional or administrative work. Duties require practical knowledge of techniques and equipment, gained through experience and/or specific training less than that represented by college graduation. This group covers positions such as electronics or engineering technician.

NASA ORGANIZATIONAL STRUCTURE

NASA is a single agency of the U.S. government comprised of a headquarters, field centers, and several specialized facilities. NASA Headquarters is located in Washington, D.C., and is responsible for interactions with Congress, the White House, and other government agencies. The headquarters staff exercises management control over the centers and other installations. Responsibilities include overseeing and developing new programs and projects; establishing management policies, procedures, and performance criteria; and evaluating the progress of all phases of the aerospace program.

NASA Headquarters
300 E Street, SW
Washington, DC 20546
Tel: +1 (202) 358-0000
http://www.nasa.gov

NASA FIELD CENTERS

Most of the technical work within NASA is performed and managed at its field centers. Located throughout the United States, each center maintains specializations and facilities in certain technical areas. Interestingly enough, the field centers overlap in their technical expertise and have been known to compete with one another for certain projects and funding.

Field Centers and Locations

• Ames Research Center	California
• Armstrong Flight Research Center	California
• Glenn Research Center	Ohio
• Goddard Space Flight Center	Maryland
• Jet Propulsion Laboratory	California
• Johnson Space Center	Texas
• Kennedy Space Center	Florida
• Langley Research Center	Virginia
• Marshall Space Flight Center	Alabama
• Stennis Space Center	Mississippi

Other Locations

• Goddard Institute for Space Studies	New York
• IV and V Facility	West Virginia
• Michoud Assembly Facility	Louisiana
• NASA Engineering and Safety Center	Virginia
• NASA Safety Center	Ohio
• NASA Shared Services Center	Mississippi
• Wallops Flight Facility	Virginia
• White Sands Test Facility	New Mexico

Ames Research Center

Ames conducts critical research and develops enabling technologies in astrobiology, information technology, fundamental space biology, nanotechnology, air traffic management, thermal protection systems, and human factors essential to virtually all NASA missions. Areas of interest include entry systems, supercomputing, airborne science, low-cost science missions to low Earth orbit and the Moon, biology and astrobiology, finding exoplanets, autonomy and robotics, lunar science, human factors, wind tunnels, and ground testing.

> Moffett Field, CA 95035
> Tel: +1 (650) 604-5000 / +1 (650) 604-4789
> http://www.nasa.gov/centers/ames/home/index.html

Armstrong Flight Research Center

As the lead for flight research, NASA Armstrong focuses on innovations in aeronautics and space technology. The newest, fastest, the highest—all have made their debut in the vast, clear desert skies over Armstrong.

> Edwards, CA 93523
> Tel: +1 (661) 276-3449
> http://www.nasa.gov/centers/armstrong/home/index.html

Glenn Research Center

Glenn Research Center develops and transfers critical technologies that address national priorities through research, technology development, and systems development for safe and reliable aeronautics, aerospace, and space applications.

Glenn's core competencies include air-breathing propulsion; communications technology and development (air traffic management, communications and navigation among satellites, aircraft, spacecraft, astronauts, robots and ground systems; advanced antennas, integrated radio frequency and optical terminals, software-defined radios, high-power amplifiers and networking for high-data-rate communications); advanced spacecraft propulsion systems and cryogenic fluid flight systems; in-space propulsion includes: propellants, chemical propulsion, and electric propulsion (ion, Hall, plasma) and nuclear propulsion; cryogenic fluid management; power, energy storage and conversion; and materials and structures for extreme environments.

> 21000 Brookpark Rd
> Cleveland, OH 44135
> Tel: +1 (216) 433-8806
> http://www.nasa.gov/centers/glenn/home/index.html

Goddard Space Flight Center

NASA's Goddard Space Flight Center is home to the nation's largest organization of combined scientists, engineers, and technologists who build spacecraft, instruments and new technology to study Earth, the Sun, the solar system, and the universe.

> 8800 Greenbelt Road
> Greenbelt, MD 20771
> Tel: +1 (301) 286-0697
> http://www.nasa.gov/centers/goddard/home/index.html

Jet Propulsion Laboratory

The Jet Propulsion Laboratory, managed by the California Institute of Technology is NASA's lead center for robotic exploration of the solar system (including *Galileo*, Voyager, *Magellan,* and upcoming missions to Mars). It also is heavily involved with environmental research (including the Shuttle Imaging Radar and TOPEX/POSEIDON).

> 4800 Oak Grove Drive
> Pasadena, CA 91109
> Tel: +1 (818) 354-5011
> http://www.nasa.gov/centers/jpl/home/index.html or
> http://www.jpl.nasa.gov

Johnson Space Center

From the early Gemini, Apollo, and Skylab projects to today's International Space Station and Orion programs, as well as home to the NASA astronaut corps, Johnson is NASA's lead center for human spaceflight and hosts mission control operations.

> 2101 NASA Road One
> Houston, TX 77058
> Tel: +1 (281) 483-5111
> http://www.nasa.gov/centers/johnson/home/index.html

Kennedy Space Center

Prepares and launches missions around Earth and beyond.

> Kennedy Space Center, FL 32899
> Tel: +1 (321) 867-2468
> http://www.nasa.gov/centers/kennedy/home/index.html

Langley Research Center

Focus areas include aeronautics, atmospheric science, space experiments, and technology spinoffs.

Hampton, VA 23681
Tel: +1 (757) 864-6110
http://www.nasa.gov/centers/langley/home/index.html

Marshall Space Flight Center

Maintains expertise in large-scale, complex space systems development with a core capability in propulsion. Involved with every stage of spacecraft and launch vehicle development and operations, including developing large space structures and their supporting space systems. Marshall also develops and manages small satellite projects and scientific payloads on a variety of spacecraft; develops, tests, and manages scientific instruments, experiments, and spacecraft that gather vital information about Earth and space; and performs microgravity research.

Huntsville, AL 35812
Tel: +1 (256) 544-0034
http://www.nasa.gov/centers/marshall/home/index.html

Stennis Space Center

Stennis is responsible for NASA's rocket propulsion testing and for partnering with industry to develop and implement remote-sensing technology.

Stennis Space Center, MS 39529
Tel: +1 (228) 688-3341
http://www.nasa.gov/centers/stennis/home/index.html

Other NASA Facilities

Goddard Institute for Space Studies

Conducts a broad study of global change, an interdisciplinary initiative addressing natural and human-made changes in the environment that occur on various time scales—one-time events, such as volcanic explosions; seasonal and annual effects, such as El Niño; and up to the millennia of ice ages—and how they affect the habitability of our planet.

2880 Broadway, New York, NY 10025
Tel: +1 (212) 678-5507
http:// www.giss.nasa.gov

IV and V Facility

NASA's Independent Verification and Validation (IV&V) Facility was established in 1993 to provide the highest achievable levels of safety and cost effectiveness for mission critical software. NASA's IV&V Program houses approximately 270 employees

100 University Drive, Fairmont, WV 26554
Tel: +1 (304) 367-8200
http://www.nasa.gov/centers/ivv/home/index.html

Michoud Assembly Facility

Michoud's capabilities include the manufacture and assembly of critical hardware components for exploration vehicles under development at Marshall and other NASA centers.

New Orleans, LA 70129
Tel: +1 (504) 257-3311
http://www.nasa.gov/centers/marshall/michoud/index.html

NASA Engineering and Safety Center

The ESC's mission is to perform value-added independent testing, analysis, and assessments of NASA's high-risk projects to ensure safety and mission success.

c/o NASA Langley Research Center
Mail Stop 118, Hampton, VA 23681
Tel: +1 (757) 864-6110
http://www.nasa.gov/offices/nesc/home/

NASA Safety Center

Established in October 2006 to support the safety and mission assurance requirements of NASA's portfolio of programs and projects. Focused on improving the development of personnel, processes, and tools needed for the safe and successful achievement of NASA's strategic goals, the NSC is comprised of four functional offices: technical excellence, knowledge management systems, audits and assessments, and mishap investigation support.

> 22800 Cedar Point Road, Cleveland, OH 44142
> Tel: +1 (440) 962-3230
> http://www.nasa.gov/offices/nsc/home/index.html

NASA Shared Services Center

The NSSC performs selected business activities for all NASA centers in financial management, human resources, information technology, procurement, and business support services. The NSSC is supported, under contract, by its service provider, CSC.

> Building 1111, C Road
> Stennis Space Center, MS 39529
> Tel: +1 (877) 677-2123
> http://www.nssc.nasa.gov/

Wallops Flight Facility

Wallops primary technical activities include launching research carriers, such as sounding rockets, balloons, aircraft, and small orbital carriers, as well as conducting Earth science research and operating the Wallops Orbital Tracking Station.

> Wallops Island, VA 23337
> Tel: +1 (757) 824-1579
> http://www.nasa.gov/centers/wallops/home/index.html

White Sands Test Facility

WSTF conducts simulated mission duty cycle testing to develop numerous full-scale propulsion systems and is a center of technical excellence in the fields of high-pressure oxygen systems/materials and rocket propellant safety. WSTF also offers functional and performance evaluation tests; hazards/failure analyses of materials, components, and complete systems; and system design evaluation and recommendations.

12600 NASA Road, Las Cruces, NM 88012
Tel: +1 (575) 524-5521
http://www.nasa.gov/centers/wstf/home/index.html

OTHER CIVIL SPACE ORGANIZATIONS

Federal Aviation Administration

The Office of Commercial Space Transportation manages its licensing and regulatory work as well as a variety of programs and initiatives to ensure the health and facilitate the growth of the U.S. commercial space transportation industry via five divisions: the Space Transportation Development Division, the Licensing and Evaluation Division, the Regulations and Analysis Division, the Safety Inspection Division, and the Operations Integration Division.

Office of Commercial Space Transportation
800 Independence Ave SW
Washington, DC 20591
Tel: +1 (202) 267-7793
http://www.faa.gov/go/ast

Federal Communications Commission

The FCC is responsible for developing and administering policies and procedures concerning the regulation of telecommunications facilities and services under its jurisdiction and licensing of satellite and radio communications activities. In addition, the FCC represents the United States in international negotiations for satellite frequency allocations. Most of the employment opportunities in the office are in the area of law and licensing.

FCC International Bureau
445 12th Street SW
Washington, DC 20554
Tel: +1 (202) 418-0437
http://www.fcc.gov/international-bureau

International Trade Administration / Department of Commerce

The ITA—Office of Transportation and Machinery's Aerospace Team, works to promote and expand opportunities for U.S. companies on the international market.

> U.S. Department of Commerce
> International Trade Administration
> Room 4036
> Washington, DC 20230-0001
> Tel: +1 (202) 482-0554
> http://www.trade.gov/td/otm/aero.asp

National Oceanic and Atmospheric Administration (NOAA)

NOAA's activities relate to the monitoring, prediction, research, and distribution of data related to the weather and the environment. Scientists at NOAA are active in research related to meteorology, oceanography, solid-earth geophysics, and solar terrestrial sciences. In addition, NOAA maintains and employs personnel for ground-station operations of satellites and archiving and distributing large databases containing research and meteorological data. Its facilities can be found throughout the United States and include the National Hurricane Center in Florida, the National Climactic Data Center in North Carolina, the Space Environment Center in Colorado, and the Satellite Operations Control Center in Maryland. The division responsible for most of NOAA's space activities is the National Environmental Satellite, Data, and Information Service (NESDIS). NESDIS maintains two primary constellations of environmental satellites: polar-orbiting and geostationary satellites. These are part of NOAA's integrated observing system, which includes satellites, radars, surface automated weather stations, weather balloons, sounders, buoys, instrumented aircraft, and other sensors, along with the data management infrastructure needed for this system.

> NESDIS Headquarters
> 1335 East-West Highway, 8th Floor
> Silver Spring, MD 20910
> Tel: +1 (301) 713-3578

Agency website: http://www.noaa.gov
NESDIS website: http://www.nesdis.noaa.gov
Agency career website: http://www.careers.noaa.gov/

National Science Foundation

NSF is an independent federal agency that aims to promote and advance scientific progress. With an annual budget of $7.2 billion (FY2014), it funds approximately 24 percent of all federally supported basic research conducted by America's colleges and universities.

National Science Foundation
4201 Wilson Blvd.
Arlington, VA 22230
Tel: +1 (703) 292-5111
Main: http://www.nsf.gov
Careers: http://www.nsf.gov/careers/

U.S. Geological Service

As the nation's largest water, Earth, and biological science and civilian mapping agency, the USGS collects, monitors, analyzes, and provides scientific understanding about natural resource conditions, issues, and problems. Among its activities are managing, using, and archiving remotely sensed geologic data and research programs in the areas of geologic mapping, tectonism, volcanism, global climate change, desert studies, exploration geology, impact crater studies, asteroid and comet radiometry, and image processing.

U.S. Geological Survey HQ
12201 Sunrise Valley Drive
Reston, VA 20192
Tel: +1 (703) 648-4460
Main: http://www.usgs.gov/
Careers: http://www.usgs.gov/ohr/

EMPLOYMENT WITHIN NASA AND THE FEDERAL GOVERNMENT

Like many large organizations, the federal government needs employees with different types of skills working in many locations. The civil agencies that we mentioned are always looking for scientists, engineers, and other talented professionals to carry forward their missions.

Changes to the federal hiring process have made it easier than in the past to apply for federal jobs, gone is the dreaded SF-171 application. But the process can still be challenging. USAJOBS.gov is the U.S. government's job portal. It is a free Web-based job board enabling access to thousands of job opportunities across hundreds of federal agencies and organizations. The Internet has made the ability to identify these much easier, however, when reviewing the positions take note of the restrictions—some jobs are limited to current government employees, some have a military veteran preference. With a generation having served in Iraq and Afghanistan and elsewhere, competition for these positions will be high. But don't get discouraged.

If you are unable to find a position within the government that meets your background and experience but would still like to work on a NASA-supported project, consider working for a private entity with a contract from NASA. Much of the work that is performed in support of NASA projects is done by contractors. For instance, the contract for the oversight and manufacturing of much of the International Space Station, resides in a contract with The Boeing Company's Defense, Space and Security Group. Likewise, the contract to develop the Orion vehicle is with Lockheed Martin.

How to Apply for a Federal Job (courtesy of Bureau of Labor and Statistics)

1. Visit USAJOBS.gov and select "U.S. Citizens" if you are a citizen who currently does not work for the federal government, or select "Federal Employees" if you currently work for the federal government.
2. Search for vacancy announcements by keywords that might describe the position you want, such as job title, occupational series, or a specific technical skill. Consider the link occupations by college major, which may give you some ideas.
3. Filter the results based on your preferences, such as agency, location, and salary. You may select these criteria from the start with the "Advanced Search" tool. You may also create automated job searches compiling daily, weekly, or monthly results.
4. Select the vacancy announcements that most interest you.

Positions within NASA

In addition to the USAJOBS.gov website, NASA has created the Staffing and Recruitment System [NASA STARS], which is integrated with the Office of Personnel Management's USAJOBS systems to streamline the application process.

- http://www.nasa.gov/about/career
- http://nasajobs.nasa.gov/

To apply for NASA job opportunities, you will need a USAJOBS account. Here are the steps to create an account:

Step 1: Create a USAJOBS account and build your résumé.

Create your account and complete your profile and build your résumé. You may create and store up to five résumés in USAJOBS. NASA's application process does not accept uploaded résumés; to apply you will need to apply with a résumé built using the USAJobs Résumé Builder. This can also be used to apply for jobs at many other federal agencies.

Step 2: Search for NASA civil service job opportunities.

You can search for NASA job opportunities by using the USAJOBS search feature available at https://nasai.usajobs.gov.

Once you have searched for and found a NASA job opportunity you are interested in, please read the vacancy announcement carefully. Take time to review your résumé to make sure you meet the eligibility and qualifications required for the position. Be sure to review the major duties of the position and ensure that your résumé describes your experience, accomplishments, education, training, and community or outside professional activities that are applicable to the position, Provide specific and detailed information including the start and end dates for each job you have held.

If you meet the eligibility requirements for the position, select the "Apply Online" button and follow the online instructions. Your information will then be transferred to NASA STARS.

Step 3: Provide additional information in NASA STARS.

Follow the online prompts to complete the application process. Be certain to read the on-screen instructions thoroughly before continuing. You will first see summary information on the job for which you are applying. Next, you will be asked to complete a series of questions that helps NASA understand your federal work experience, if any, and eligibility for special hiring authorities. When you have answered all the additional questions required, you will be asked to review your application before submitting.

Please be sure to read the announcement in its entirety before you apply to ensure you complete all the required steps and submit any supporting documentation required. You will not be considered for a position if any part of your application is incomplete.

After successfully completing the application process, you will be redirected to USAJOBS where you can view your application status, continue to search for job opportunities, or apply for additional vacancies. You may return at any time to update or make changes to your application package anytime prior to midnight EST on the closing date of the announcement.

THE U.S. MILITARY SPACE SECTOR

The military use of space preceded the establishment of NASA in 1958. However, it was not until the National Space Policy of 1978 that the military perspective and use of space was emphasized publicly as national policy. From the earliest days of the space program, the military has had a vital interest in the development of space systems. In the 1940s and 1950s, the military led the effort to develop and use the V2 rocket technology, developed by Germany for use in World War II, in U.S. missiles and rockets. In fact, the early rockets used by NASA for human spaceflight were derived from military missile designs.

Military uses of space include the utilization of satellites for:
- Communications
- Remote sensing of the environment for terrain modeling, meteorology, and oceanography
- Reconnaissance and surveillance
- Position and navigation determination
- Early warning of missile launches

In addition, the military takes an active role in:
- Launch operations
- Space systems operations
- New technology research and development

The U.S. Department of Defense's efforts are coordinated by several agencies. The Pentagon is responsible for developing an overall architecture for the space needs of the various military operations. Space Command, a joint military organization comprised of the Air Force, Army, and Navy and headquartered in Colorado Springs, Colorado, is responsible for the overall maintenance and operations of the military's space assets. These assets include satellites and their launching, ground facilities and launch pads for the rockets, and ground networks to monitor the satellites and receive data from them. Each of the component commands—Air Force, Army, Navy, etc.—also has operations devoted to the utilization of space assets, which largely depend on the mission of the command. For example, the Navy is interested in the use of remotely sensed data for oceanography and determining sea conditions, while the Army has an extensive interest in using satellites to track troop movements and equipment on the ground.

Other agencies within the military or intelligence communities that are involved with utilizing, performing research in, or developing space assets include the National Reconnaissance Office, the National Security Agency, the National Geospatial Intelligence Agency, the Missile Defense Agency, and the Central Intelligence Agency.

Finding a Space Job in the Military

Positions within the military sector are occupied not only by military personnel but also by civilian personnel directly employed by the military or by civilian contractors. For active military personnel, available positions can be found through normal command channels. Others interested in opportunities in the military should contact their local recruiting office. Civilian opportunities can be found via the same sources listed under civil government opportunities, in particular USAJobs.gov, which is the Office of Personnel Management's consolidated listing of federal job opportunities, located at: USAJOBS.gov.

You can also check the website for careers with the U.S. Air Force and the Navy.

> http://www.airforce.com/careers/
> http://www.navy.com/careers.html

THE ACADEMIC SECTOR

As would be expected, universities and non-profit research institutions are primarily involved with research. Study topics span the spectrum from the effect of microgravity on materials or biomedical drugs to new methods for improving propulsion efficiencies to evaluating sensor data on the chemical analysis of stars.

In addition to pure research, many academic organizations also develop instruments and other hardware to support their research endeavors. Research positions within the academic sector are usually reserved for faculty and university staff and therefore often require a doctoral degree (PhD).

Research within this sector is primarily funded by government sources, such as NASA, the Department of Defense, and the National Science Foundation, or by private industry. NASA maintains a mission to fund research and annually awards more than $600 million dollars to universities and non-profit research institutions.

Organizations in the Academic Sector can be found in Chapter 6: Colleges and Universities.

THE COMMERCIAL SPACE SECTOR

Commercial space has been defined as those projects or programs in which the commercial entity has acted as the lead in the financing of a new venture. In practice, however, with many companies focusing on both commercial and government clients, the commercial sector also includes all those private or public corporations that derive their revenues from government contracts but whose employees are private sector workers.

Institutions that focus only on government clients are commonly known as government contractors. The two largest and most recognizable names are known for developing and manufacturing space hardware: Boeing and Lockheed Martin. Still, there are an estimated 2,000 organizations involved with space and satellites, many playing a vital role. And like the rest of the U.S. economy, small and mid-size companies play a major role in the economic activity of the sector and represent the major area of job growth.

When we include contractors, the commercial sector tackles a large percentage of the activity within the sector, including almost all the manufacturing. Within this sector is an entire network of firms— from manufacturers and suppliers, to distributors and marketers of the product or resource, to those that provide technical and professional support.

For instance, to place a communications satellite in orbit requires companies that assemble the launch vehicle; manufacture the components (fuel pumps, tank structure, etc.) and subcomponents (gaskets, seals, valves, etc.), which make up the launch vehicle; provide test personnel to make sure the vehicle will operate correctly; provide ground-launch personnel to monitor the vehicle prior to and during flight; systems integrators that mate the payload to the vehicle, or the drivers who supply the tanks with fuel at the launch site. Then, of course, there are all the positions associated with designing, building, testing, or evaluating the satellite, the components within the satellite, and the payload, which is the reason to put the craft in orbit in the first place. And once the satellite reaches orbit, there are support personnel who will continually monitor the performance of the satellite and the end user of the data stream. Whew! But there's more.

Other organizations that would have an interest in this flight would be risk evaluators, who provide the insurance on the vehicle and the satellite; the financiers who funded the project; the market researchers who evaluated the system's potential; and the marketing personnel who sell the data derived from the satellite.

In particular, the commercial sector is being driven by orders from companies providing information, communications, and entertainment (ICE). In other words, the streaming data and video over the Internet, distributing television and radio programming to cable head ends or end-users; and global communications—anywhere and anytime on Earth. These "ICE" services are the core to the commercial sector and generate more than $150 billion annually in services enabled by satellite technology. That makes satellite services one of the largest industries in the world. And if anyone thinks it's an "outdated" solution, one need only to look at Google, Facebook, Space-X, and Microsoft, that are pitching new multibillion satellite broadband networks to spread the Internet to remote areas of the globe.

Of course, when it comes to excitement and buzz, the media is fascinated by the efforts of private companies pushing the envelope of human spaceflight, whether it is the space tourism efforts undertaken by the X-Prize, Scaled Composites and the pioneering work of Burt Rutan, Sir Richard Branson's Virgin Galactic, or XCOR; new rockets to supply the *International Space Station*, such as SpaceX and Orbital Sciences; rockets to take people to the Moon and Mars, such as Lockheed Martin's Orion, and that suggested by Elon Musk, or efforts to visit heavenly bodies, be they asteroids or the Google Lunar X-Prize to land private spacecraft on the Moon.

Where Are They Located?

The space and satellite industry is comprised of a highly diversified set of activities. While spread across the United States, like other industries, space organizations tend to concentrate in areas where the money is or near talent at larger institutions or universities. Many of the companies involved with space infrastructure historically have been based in California, Texas, Colorado, Florida, and the Washington, D.C., area.—areas close to major NASA and military research and/or operational facilities. But when you look at companies that are involved with transmitting satellite communications and video programming or analyzing remotely sensed imagery and data, you find that companies such as these are scattered throughout the nation and the world. Sometime firms are near their primary customers, other times it is simply where the president of the company set up shop.

WORKING IN THE SPACE INDUSTRY

Biography & Advice

Name	Dino Lorenzini
Organization	SpaceQuest
Job Title	CEO & Satellite Engineer
Location	Vienna, Virginia
Link	http://www.spacequest.com

Responsibilities
As the leader of a small entrepreneurial company, I am responsible for articulating the vision of the company, setting the strategic direction, and bringing together the people, partners, resources, and financing needed to turn the vision into reality.

Degrees/School
B.S. Engineering Science, US Air Force Academy
S.M. Astronautical Engineering, MIT
Sc.D. Astronautical Engineering, MIT
MBA, Auburn University

Career Path
I began my career as an Astronautical Development Engineer in the Air Force with increasing responsibilities for the management of space programs. I finished my 23-year career in the Air Force as the Program Manager for DARPA's space-based laser program and as Director of the Space Systems Architecture Study for the Strategic Defense Initiative Program. In 1989, I made the transition into commercial space to become a part of a revolutionary movement of lower cost systems with unlimited business potential. I have worked primarily with low-Earth orbit communications satellite systems as the chief architect, system designer, business developer, and promoter.

Why Space?
I chose space over aviation because I was impressed by the accomplishments of the first astronauts during my college studies, motivated by the challenge to be creative and innovative, and inspired by the national importance and significance of the U.S. space effort at that time.

Words of Wisdom
Try to think outside of the box, don't accept negative responses, be persistent in the pursuit of your dreams, and work hard.

CHOOSING THE SPACE CAREER FOR YOU

In this chapter:

We explore the various activities that make up the space industry and provide you with sample job descriptions.

You've graduated. Congratulations! A career is one of the most important life decisions you will make. You will likely spend the next 40 years working—that's more than 80,000 hours—so your job should be something you enjoy doing; something you are passionate about. Luckily, today's workforce offers greater flexibility for most people than it did in the past.

Some thoughts for you to consider:
- Pursue your interest.
- Find topics that engage you.
- Identify your skills and how they fit with what you are interested in.
- Tap into your dreams.

- Do you want to explore the unknown by working on the spaceships of tomorrow or scanning the stars for interesting phenomena?
- Do you prefer jobs with more customer interaction, such as government relations, space tourism, or satellite telecom, radio, TV, and Internet sales?
- Do you prefer a lab environment, an office, or do you want to be in the field?

Major sectors of the industry include:

- **Infrastructure:** building satellites and spacecraft, rockets and launch vehicles, ground equipment and operations, human spaceflight activities, software, new horizons

- **"ICE" Services:** satellites that provide access to information and the Internet, communications, and entertainment (television, radio)

- **Data Services:** remote sensing, geographical information systems (GIS), and Global Positioning System (GPS)

- **Science and Research:** microgravity, space science and astrophysics, and medical and biotechnology

- **Business and Administrative**

Cross-Reference Table:
Educational Degree vs. Industry Opportunities

Sector / Degree	Satellite Manufacturing	Ground Segment	Instrument Design	Launch Vehicles	Remote Sensing	Microgravity	Space Science	Human Flight
Electrical Engineering	X	X	X	X		X	X	X
Mechanical Engineering	X	X	X	X		X	X	X
Propulsion	X			X			X	X
Power	X							X
Control Systems	X	X		X		X		X
Software	X	X		X	X		X	X
Information Technology	X	X		X	X		X	X
Chemical Engineering				X		X		
Materials			X	X		X	X	
Thermal Control	X		X	X		X		X
Optics			X		X			
Structures	X			X				X
Systems Integration	X	X		X		X		X
Biology			X			X	X	X
Astrophysics			X				X	
Marketing and Sales	X	X	X	X	X	X	X	X
Legal	X	X	X	X	X	X	X	X
Public Affairs	X	X	X	X	X	X	X	X

So that you can make an informed decision, let's look at the various sectors and some of the jobs they offer.

INFRASTRUCTURE
SATELLITE DESIGN AND MANUFACTURING—BUILDING THE BRAINS

With a high demand for communications satellites and other spacecraft, companies involved with the assembly and integration of satellites and the manufacture and design of satellite components are extremely busy. Many have indicated that they are having trouble finding enough employees to fill demand. Based on the number of potential orders that have been announced, they expect to have this problem for the foreseeable future. The satellite manufacturing sector is dependent on a number of factors, including the ability of their potential customers to secure the financing needed to build, launch, and operate their satellites. Not every venture reaches fruition. In addition, like most sectors requiring an asset that is used over a period of years, the order and delivery of spacecraft can be cyclical. However, this should not affect employment within the broader sector as the long-range forecast shows steady growth and a long-term need for trained and qualified workers.

The Importance of Satellites

Satellites are the primary driver of the space industry today, providing a means to generate or transmit data and information across great distances. From orbits above Earth, satellites:

- Transmit voice, data, and facsimiles across the globe.
- Enable mobile telecommunications across vast regions of Earth.
- Provide remote areas of the world with the infrastructure to access telecommunications and the Internet at lower costs.
- Transmit and relay visual images for television and cable programming distribution, medical imaging and telemedicine capabilities, and tele-education services, including distance learning.
- Monitor and predict the Earth's weather.
- Monitor the Earth's environment.

- Enable reconnaissance and surveillance from vast distances, whether for military or scientific purposes looking at the Earth or to the sky above.

How Satellites Work?

The primary components within a satellite are the:

- **Bus**—The electronic brain of the satellite, which processes and monitors all functions of the satellite.

- **Body**—The physical structure, which holds or supports the other components.

- **Power Supply**—For Earth-orbiting satellites, this generally consists of solar cells in an array and a storage device such as a battery. Other types of power supplies include nuclear devices (usually for interplanetary missions) or fuel cells for storage.

- **Antennas and Associated Electronic Equipment**—To receive, amplify, and transmit information.

- **Sensor Package**—For remote-sensing applications this could include devices to measure solar radiation, imagery of the Earth's surface, or the local temperature of the ocean's surface.

Employees working in this field use electronics and/or computers to design, develop, manufacture, and test the various systems that make up a satellite. Because the satellite will operate in an environment where repairs are difficult, if not impossible, to make, quality is an extremely important issue. Much of the hardware assembly and manufacturing takes place in a clean room to prevent dust and other particles from contaminating the system.

Technical positions include those that relate to the following:

- Bus Design
- Structure Design and Manufacturing
- System Integration
- Sensor Design
- Satellite Power Systems
- On-Board Software and Hardware
- Quality Control

Sample Classified Ads and Position Descriptions for
Satellite Manufacturing

Spacecraft Preliminary Design Engineer

Electrical engineering position involved with spacecraft design and fabrication and spacecraft electronics systems design. Responsible for spacecraft preliminary designs, mission payload and spacecraft electronics design, and tradeoff analyses. Lead front-end spacecraft and ground-segment design effort. Familiarity with spacecraft attitude control systems and digital processor and telemetry/command subsystems and their interactions.

Satellite Digital Design Engineer

Design, test, and integration tasks. Some analog circuit design and spacecraft experience desirable. Proficient in designs utilizing microprocessors, associated memory, I/O, and controller circuitry.

Jr. Digital Design Engineer

Perform spacecraft design, test, and integration tasks focusing on real-time design in satellite command, ranging, and telemetry subsystems.

Mission Planning Engineer

Participate in spacecraft satellite operations planning and development of the spacecraft control center software and operational hardware, while supporting mission operations and related activities, such as prelaunch integration, post-launch checkout, and deployment of satellites.

Systems Engineer

Spacecraft systems and systems design with experience in both electrical and mechanical subsystems, electric power, propulsion, ADACS, thermal, and ground subsystems through integration and test.

Principal Mechanical Engineer

Responsible for the design, fabrication, integration, and testing of spacecraft structural and mechanical components, and electromechanical systems and components. Experience in design verification, document production and analysis, cost analysis, design, test and manufacturing support, and planning.

Power Engineer

Responsible for the design of electric power conversion and control equipment, including analysis, circuit design, electrical layout, prototyping, production support, test, and system integration.

Systems Engineer

Familiarity with all spacecraft electronics subsystems and communications payloads required. Experience with preliminary design and analyses, advanced concepts, proven as well as advanced technology, and hands-on experience at the satellite/payload component design, fabrication, and test and integration level.

Lead Engineer

Geosynchronous attitude determination and controls, including experience in attitude control, spin axis attitude determination, analysis and simulation, and flight software specification/test support.

Satellite RF/Microwave Engineer

Geostationary satellite experience with design and development of C-band, S-band, and other microwave frequency satellite communications hardware from design through integration. Proficient in communications analysis and circuit design and analysis in the S through Ku band, part selection, space qualification test, and subsystem and system integration and test.

Senior Engineering Technician

Responsible for building test fixtures, testing spacecraft components, and supporting engineering by assisting in the fabrication of breadboards. Field experience preferred. Ability to read and understand schematic diagrams and troubleshoot analog and digital circuits.

Flight Software Engineers

Develop onboard navigation, control, and communications software systems. Programming embedded in computers and other common devices.

Manager, Satellite Payload Engineer

Manage payload design, development, integration, and test.

Electronics Technicians

Integrate and test components for satellite ground stations and gateway centers.

INFRASTRUCTURE
LAUNCH VEHICLES—PROVIDING ACCESS TO SPACE

The expendable launch vehicle, which is based on the missile technologies of the 1950s, is the mainstay of the space industry for placing payloads in orbit. Vehicles, such as the Delta, Atlas, and Titan, have been hurling payloads into space on a regular basis since the 1960s.

In addition to the above, a range of expendable vehicles, which are available on the market today, are capable of launching small, medium, intermediate, or heavy payloads (4,000+ kg). Among these are a number from international sources. In addition to the above vehicles are the Ariane (Europe), Proton and Angara (Russia), Long March (China), Minotaur (U.S.), Pegasus (U.S.), Falcon (U.S.) ,and dozens of other vehicles capable of launching a payload into orbit or a suborbital trajectory. In the past few years there has also been the emergence of several "air launch" concepts that can lob satellites into orbit.

With a need to put payloads into orbit for communications, Earth-monitoring, science missions, and military needs, launch vehicles can be booked several years in advance. The driving forces for the industry continue to be the dual mantra of increased reliability and cost reduction. Every launch vehicle manufacturer. seeks to improve its performance and reliability and reduce payload losses. With the competitive nature of the industry, these companies undergo a constant evaluation process to reduce costs, improve profit margins, and provide a better price to their customers.

Throughout the years, a number of companies have sought to gain a foothold in the launch market, and it is a continually evolving activity. Today SpaceX, Orbital Sciences, Boeing, Sierra Nevada, and others, are joining firms such as Lockheed Martin and Boeing and developing vehicles that can transport payloads into space for humans and cargo.

This should not affect your choice in a career or a company. Keep in mind the following: new vehicles do not quickly replace existing ones; they will coexist for a number of years. Likewise, not every vehicle will succeed in its development. But the skills applicable to one vehicle are generally applicable to the others. The manufacture and launch of rockets is an employment-intensive business that requires a skilled workforce.

Launch Vehicle Components

A launch vehicle is made up of several major pieces of hardware:
- Engine
- Fuel
- Support structure, including fuel and/or oxidizer tanks
- Fairing

Of these, the fairing is probably the least familiar term, but it is one of the most critical pieces of hardware. The fairing is the part of the rocket that attaches the payload to the launch vehicle and allows it to release the payload into the proper orbit. Part of the fairing is a separation device that allows this to occur. If the fairing does not operate as designed, then the payload might be damaged or left in a useless orbit. In both cases, the mission would be a failure.

Jobs in This Area

Most of the labor in the launch vehicle industry is related to the design, development, manufacture, and test of the vehicle. Positions range from technicians in a machine shop or assembly floor to engineers designing subsystems, solving assembly problems, or overseeing test operations. As an employee, you might be involved in one of the following areas:

- Manufacturing—Components & Structures
- Component and Vehicle Testing
- Quality Control
- Engineering—Materials, Propulsion, Structures, Control Systems, Thermal Analysis
- Drafting/CAD Design
- Aerodynamics
- Propellant Testing & Development

Sample Classified Ads and Position Descriptions for
Launch Vehicle Personnel

Thermal Engineer

Develop large thermal models of space vehicles using highly specialized computer software programs.

Propulsion Engineer

Participate in the design, development, integration, test, and evaluation of propulsion-related activities. Background in cryogenic and/or hyperbolic propulsion systems. Strong background in propulsion component (valves and regulators) design for turbo machinery.

Propulsion Systems Engineer

Opportunities exist in the conversion of energy into power for space systems. Specializations include liquid propulsion systems, solid propulsion systems, electrical propulsion and power, energy conversion, nuclear energy processes, nuclear propulsion and power, chemical energy processes, internal flow dynamics, and propulsion system dynamics.

Vehicle System Engineer

From mission planning through launch operations, the Integration and Test Operations Group has a variety of exciting opportunities for engineers with hands-on hardware experience. Requires excellent organizational skills and the ability to work in a technical team.

Astrodynamics

Design and calculate the formulas and perturbations that determine a satellite's trajectory or orbit. Requires extensive mathematics and computer skills.

Draftsperson/Computer Aided Design

Draw sketches and schematics of systems, subsystems, and hardware to specifications provided by the engineers.

Materials and Structures

Positions involved with research, design, development, test, and evaluation (RDDT&E) of aerospace vehicle structures and the study of their behavior in flight regimes. These positions are also engaged in research into the behavior and characteristics of materials for use in flight vehicles and systems. Included in this group are the following specialties: materials, structural mechanics, aerospace metals, basic properties of materials, polymers, refractory compounds, friction and lubrication, structural mechanics, and flight structures. Majors include ceramics or ceramic engineering, metallurgy or metallurgical engineering, physics, engineering (various), and chemistry.

Fluid and Flight Mechanics

Positions concerned with the study and investigation of dynamics of aerospace vehicle flight and the establishment of criteria for aerospace vehicle design based on the dynamics of flight. Positions may also be concerned with the investigation of the interaction of the vehicle in flight and the environment. Positions are also engaged with research, development, design, test, and evaluation of systems to guide and control the vehicle in flight. Specializations in this group include flight mechanics, control and guidance systems, fluid mechanics, magnetofluid dynamics, aerostructural dynamics, vehicle acoustics, heat transfer, stability, control and performance, flight vehicle atmosphere environment, and basis properties of gases.

INFRASTRUCTURE
GROUND OPERATIONS

Launch Operations / Spaceports

Launch vehicles are operated and tested at specialized facilities that contain the necessary support infrastructure. In addition to the launch pad, the site generally contains a ground station area to monitor the launch, a payload processing facility where the payloads are mated to the fairing in the launch vehicle, and any number of storage tanks containing fuel, oxygen, and oxidizers. Many of the employees work in areas related to safety, test, ground control operations, electrical and mechanical support, and construction and facility design.

Over the past few years, spaceports now dot the United States and can be eyed as growing enterprises and hubs of space-related career opportunities. As example, in 2014, the FAA approved a commercial space launch site license for the Midland, Texas International Air & Space Port. XCOR Aerospace plans to launch suborbital flights from that site. Similarly, SpaceX received key environmental approval from the FAA for a proposed commercial spaceport launch site in south Texas.

In a related development, New Mexico's Spaceport America has posted job opportunities at that complex, in preparation for handling Virgin Galactic's space tourism efforts and other customers making use of their facilities.

For an informative guide to spaceports and other helpful data, visit: http://www.faa.gov/about/office_org/headquarters_offices/ast/medi a/2014-02-04_FAA_2013_Compendium.pdf

Sample Classified Ads and Position Descriptions for
Launch Vehicle Operations

Experimental Facilities and Equipment

Includes the design, development, test, evaluation, operation, and management of aerospace research-and-development facilities, and equipment for experimental and operational purposes. Positions include the following specialties: launch and flight operations, experimental tooling and equipment, fluid and flow dynamics, electrical experimental equipment, and experimental facilities techniques.

Flight Systems

Positions in this specialty are concerned with systems integration, reliability studies, evaluation of systems and subsystems design and performance characteristics. Included in this specialty are positions performing research, development and evaluation of manufacturing and quality assurance programs. The following specialties are included in this group: reliability, flight systems test, experimental manufacturing techniques, quality assurance, electrical systems, and piloted spaceflight systems.

Air Force Missile and Space Systems Electronic Maintenance Specialist

It takes skill, expertise, and attention to detail to maintain and program missiles, rockets, and remotely piloted aircraft. The job entails monitoring, operating, and supervising operation of consoles, fault display panels, and checkout equipment and also the disassemble, inspect, service, and replacement of components and wiring.

* * *

Satellite Operations

Positions involved with satellite operations include the following activities:

- Monitoring the vital signs of a spacecraft and performing the real-time analysis of the health of the satellite
- Operating ground-station hardware for processing of data
- Developing software for planning the satellite and

evaluating onboard performance and operations
- Receiving and transmitting data to and from satellites for communications or remote monitoring of Earth

Use of Satellite Ground Stations
The ground station is used to receive data that originates from a satellite. Two types of data are received. The first is used for station keeping of the satellite to determine if it is operating within expected parameters. The second is the data that the satellite has been sent up for —telephone calls, remotely sensed imagery, etc.

Remotely sensed data, which is transmitted from the satellite, is stored on disk and recorded by time index and any other variables that are determined to be of necessity. Communications data is sent from the ground station to a local network, where the data can be sent via the ground or through another satellite to its intended destination.

Sample Classified Ads and Position Descriptions for Ground Segment Personnel

Satellite Control Operators

Responsible for the daily operation of the ground system required to support satellite control functions. Duties include routine satellite and ground station monitoring and control, response to satellite and ground system anomalies, and collection reporting of all satellite and ground station activities. Experience in any of the following is desired: satellite communications terminal operation/maintenance, communications network operation, or computer operations.

Mission Control Operators

These individuals will operate the mission control systems for configuring payload, maintaining the quality of the satellite broadcast, and controlling all access to the satellite by feeder link Earth stations. The controllers will be responsible for the restoration of broadcast services in the event of satellite failures or impairment in the space segment.

Air Force Space Systems Operator

Operating the largest space program in the world takes the combined efforts and skills of thousands of Airmen, especially Space Systems Operations specialists. These experts are responsible for everything from detecting sea-launched ballistic missiles and tracking satellites to assisting in rocket launches and spaceflight operations.

Air Force Space and Missile Operations Office

From missiles that safely eliminate distant targets to satellites that enhance our communication and tracking, Space and Missile Operations officers direct the entire system. They oversee surveillance, missile launch, space lift, ballistic space warning, and satellite command and control. They also formulate policies, perform inspections, establish organizational structure, and determine the personnel required to support mission areas. By assessing the effectiveness of all space and missile operations and incorporating new technology as it becomes available, they develop future plans for system, facilities, and personnel.

Senior Operations System Support Engineer

Participate in operational issue investigations and resolutions working with internal and external resources (i.e., employees, vendors, and contractors) to resolve and prevent issues in network management systems and security information management systems. Administers network management systems.

* * *

Ground Stations and Equipment

The ground segment of the industry is comprised of a diverse group of companies that manufacture electronic equipment necessary to make use of the satellites in orbit. More organizations are involved in this aspect of the industry, in particular those manufacturing equipment for use in communications, information, and entertainment. These can range from a large several-meter antenna dish to ones small enough for an apartment balcony; sophisticated trucks containing a variety of electronic equipment to a chipset used to access the GPS signal for a cell phone. More people are involved in the ground-segment manufacturing than those for spacecraft and launch vehicles. It is a major source for industry revenue and employment. In fact, it is several times larger than the revenues generated for building spacecraft and rockets.

Among the many functions of the ground segment are:

- Designing, developing, manufacturing, and testing electronic components that make up the ground station, including the antennas, relays, amplifiers, modulators, etc.
- GPS devices from chipsets to stand alone and integrated devices
- Receivers that enable consumers to access video and radio
- Receivers that enable consumers and businesses to access broadband
- Portable and transportable systems to enable communications in the air, at sea, and in remote areas.
- The design and assembly of launch, test, and operations facilities
- Developing data storage and archive retrieval hardware and software

Commercial and military applications have expanded rapidly during the past decade and this growth is constantly evolving. As the need to make use of the latest electronics and technologies that enable access to satellite television, radio, and broadband or communications in the sky and oceans, the space industry continues to need engineers to keep them at the forefront.

Sample Classified Ads and Position Descriptions for
Ground Equipment Personnel

Principal Radiofrequency (RF) Network Engineer

Responsible for providing engineering and sustaining engineering of RF solutions for RF/ antenna communications services, carrier monitoring systems and TT&C (Telemetry, Tracking & Command) infrastructure. The design of these solutions take into account the appropriate redundancy, availability, scalability, and manageability requirements for RF systems that support spacecraft Telemetry, Tracking and Command (TT&C), In-Orbit Testing (IOT), and Transfer Orbit Support Services (TOSS) global services.

Principal Engineer, Integration & Testing

The primary responsibility of the candidate is to perform Systems/Integration testing of complex real-time satellite ground network systems designed to monitor and command the Intelsat fleet of satellites.

Measurement and Instrumentation

Develop systems to measure and record physical phenomena and information to control environments and processes by means of various types of instrumentation, e.g., electrical, electronic, mechanical, and combinations. This work includes tracking systems, telemetry, radio, optical, and mechanical systems and subsystems. Included in this group are sensors and transducers, heat and light measurement, measurement standards and calibration, automated control systems, and the electronics of materials.

Software Engineer—Ground Station

Develop workstation spacecraft command-and-control systems. Individuals will develop real-time command-and-control services, graphical user interface display services, orbit, and attitude applications. Orbital analysis requires experience with orbital mechanics and simulation of dynamic systems.

Very Small Aperature Teerminal (VSAT) Implementation Specialists

Requires knowledge of VSAT hardware and systems, RF and IF systems, building construction practices, and VSAT installation types and procedures.

VSAT Applications Engineer

Familiarity with data communications protocols.

Antenna Engineers

Design, fabrication, and test of UHF and microwave antenna systems. Knowledge of phase-tracked spiral antennas for interferometer arrays desired. Knowledge of analytical tools to support antenna design and installation interactions, including method of moments and geometrical theory of diffraction-based codes.

Antenna Engineer

Responsible for performing feed/antenna design analyses, including efficiency, gain, and radiation patterns of the feed as well as the antenna. Performs microwave systems analyses including dynamic range, noise figure, gain/loss and intermodulation and antenna noise temperature G/T and EIRP calculations. Supports IR&D development proposals as well as program execution.

Communications Test Engineer

Compose test procedures, configure test hardware, and perform tests on RF and communications equipment for spacecraft and launch vehicles. Knowledge of communications theory principles and experience with digital data transmission systems characterization.

Military Satellite Communications Technician

Support the installation, operation, and maintenance of enterprise and tactical satellite communications networks, terminals, and associated equipment in Ka-band, X-band, C-band, Ku-band, EHF, and UHF frequency ranges. Monitor and analyze satellite communications links and identify and rectify performance issues. Perform troubleshooting and repair of high-power amplifiers, fiber-optic systems, up converters, down converters, RF switching units, antenna control units, low-noise amplifiers, and low-noise block down converters and switching and monitoring audio and video equipment. Perform fault isolation and diagnostic assessment and execution of corrective actions on real-time basis.

DSP Systems Engineer

Provide design direction and oversight to experienced software, firmware, RF and test engineers to develop signal processing solutions for SATCOM/terrestrial customers. Projects range from a single chassis to complex racks at multiple worldwide sites.

INFRASTRUCTURE
HUMAN SPACEFLIGHT ACTIVITIES

Positions involved with human spaceflight have historically been driven by NASA. Activities involve developing control devices and hardware to keep the crew alive and functioning. In addition to the above hardware, government-sponsored research is performed on methods to evaluate and improve human conditions in space with respect to the physical and psychological problems faced by crews during long missions.

Mission Hardware

The most important hardware and software associated with human spaceflight are the life support systems for the vehicles as well as those for extravehicular activities. While the most familiar piece of hardware is the spacesuit, systems to control oxygen levels and waste removal are extremely vital. Other hardware used in human space travel applications relate to cooking, bathing, and cleaning. Most of the new devices are funded by government either by NASA, International Space Station partners in Europe and Japan, or organizations in Russia or China.

INFRASTRUCTURE
OTHER EXAMPLES

SOFTWARE, TEST, AND INFORMATION TECHNOLOGY

Almost any software or information technology skill that exists in the broader economy can be found in the space industry. Skilled people are needed in network management, database design and development, object-oriented techniques, software integration and test, software architecture and design, scientific/analysis software, flight software development, and spacecraft and ground systems software development.

Sample Classified Ads and Position Descriptions

Software Engineer

Develop reusable real-time embedded software for satellite systems. Perform detailed design, coding, and testing of software units. Support software subsystem integration. Requires a B.S. degree in computer science, math, physics, electrical engineering, or related field and knowledge of advanced software programming languages.

Software Engineer

Basic duties involve attitude control system design, analysis, and simulation. Tasks include working for senior engineers in the areas of spacecraft attitude control, control system stability analysis, control law design, system hardware component modeling and analysis, and system-level performance analysis. Knowledge of C programming language and computer-aided simulation software.

Software Engineer

Conduct analyses and designs in one of the following orbit, mission, and system analysis disciplines: ascent trajectory generation, launch system performance, orbital transfer, constellation coverage, multi-body relative motion, coverage, orbit ephemeris generation and determination, orbit perturbation modeling, mission operations, and reentry.

Sr. Software Engineer

Perform science data analysis. Work closely with scientists in data reduction and analysis. Maintain instrument operations software, including data maintenance, distribution of science data, database management, and operations management.

Hardware and Software System Engineering

A system engineer to perform a wide range of hardware and software prototype and analysis activities to analyze options for future satellite communications systems. Works with both hardware (e.g., cabling equipment together, using test equipment, such as meters and oscilloscopes) and software (e.g., installing operating systems, developing code, testing and debugging software).

Software Development Engineer

Develop, integrate, and test real-time software and GUI applications to support various satellite ground station products (e.g., modems, gateways, front end processors, etc.) Use C/C++, HTML5, Flash, and Python software tools to develop solutions for various Linux based platforms.

EXAMPLES OF SOME OTHER TECHNICAL POSITIONS

- **Quality Assurance Technician or Engineer**—All systems that must function in space require that the risk due to faulty hardware or software be kept at an absolute minimum (many subsystems require 99.999 percent reliability or better). Material tolerances are to sub-fractions of an inch.

People in these positions are responsible for establishing and maintaining a quality assurance program, including subcontract/vendor control, incoming inspection, in-process inspection, process controls, integration/test support, qualification/ acceptance test definitions, and database development.

- **Analyst**—Consulting positions that provide guidance and expertise to a client, usually to determine the best possible solution or the effect of a suggested solution.

- **Systems Architecture Studies**—A limited number of positions within the industry are available for developing the requirements necessary for achieving a goal, such as the necessary space systems for military operations and long-range planning related to lunar bases and Mars missions. Many of these positions are in the military or at NASA and universities.

INFRASTRUCTURE

NEW HORIZONS

During the next several decades, expanded commercial use of space is expected. Growth of telecommunications satellite services, including navigation, disaster warning, fleet dispatch, and emergency location will spawn 21st-century firms specializing in customer products. Earth remote-sensing products tailored to a customer's interests will become widespread around the globe—so too will navigation, detection, and tracking services.

Eventually, advances in launch systems should bring about more routine and far less costly access to space. If so, more commercial firms are likely to find business niches in Earth orbit. Mining, manufacturing, power generation, and hazardous waste processing, have all been proposed. A new, next generation of launchers could one day herald airline-like space operations. This would be a major step forward in reducing the cost of placing payloads and people into orbit. Some experts predict a large, blossoming space tourism travel business! Privately operated spaceliners may drop off passengers at "get away from it all" recreational and resort facilities in low-Earth orbit. This is not a farfetched vision if the expense of lofting a passenger drops to the same level as taking a luxury ocean cruise. Given the pioneering spirit that opened up previous frontiers on Earth, our newest arena for economic expansion may be as unbounded as space itself.

SATELLITE SERVICES
INFORMATION, COMMUNICATIONS, AND ENTERTAINMENT (ICE)

The rapid growth of services providing communications and the distribution and access to information (such as the Internet) and entertainment (such as video and audio programming) is the driving force behind the industry's growth during the past 25 years. Satellites provide an instant infrastructure across geographically disperse areas and enable companies to provide services quickly, securely, and, in many cases, less expensively than building a fiber, wireless, or cable network. Initially satellites provided an easy means to distribute video from one location to multiple locations (one to many) and provide backup to voice and private data networks. The growth of the Internet and video streaming and an ever-increasing need for more bandwidth has only increased the need for satellites, which have become a vital element of an integrated data network as well as an effective solution for reaching customers and businesses directly in competition with terrestrial alternatives.

Among the satellite-based services that are provided are:

- Fixed satellite services, allowing the broadcast and redistribution of television and cable programming to cable head ends
- Direct-to-consumer television and radio broadcasting
- Mobile telephony services providing users access to communications and information—whether over the ocean, in the mountains, in remote areas, or onboard an aircraft

- International voice and data traffic
- High-speed Internet access to homes and businesses
- Store-and-forward communications, which allow a remote or mobile site to transmit or receive data or location information, such as text messages, electric utility usage, or locations for a trucking fleet
- Transmission of medical data and information on private data networks
- Transmission of educational programming on private data networks

Among the companies involved with the space-based telecommunications sector are satellite providers, such as Intelsat, Inmarsat, SES Global, Telesat, Iridium, and Globalstar; private networks and satellite broadband firms, such as Hughes/Echostar and Viasat; companies that use satellites to distribute their programming, such as HBO, Showtime, or Discover networks; and teleport operators, such as Harris CapRock, Globecomm, or Encompass Digital Media, that provide uplink and downlink services.

Careers in This Area

Engineers specializing in this field, work toward system optimizations. They develop ways to transmit and receive more information in less time and over greater distances; mobile systems that use less power and reduce the size and weight of ground equipment; and networks to transmit data seamless across satellite, ground, and wireless networks.

Because of their connection to B2B or B2C (business to business or consumer) services, this sector hires a large number of employees who may not be technical sales, marketing, customer service personnel.

Sample Classified Ads and Position Descriptions

Network Communications Engineer

Network/communications engineer with experience with small aperture terminals (VSAT) and larger fixed ground-station satellite systems operating in a variety of industry standard SATCOM network configurations to include SCPC, TDMA, etc., and logistics. Responsibilities include site surveys for install of fixed and mobile SATCOM terminals to include power, space, look angle, frequency management, and other install considerations; and coordination with vendors of SATCOM service and SATCOM hardware to engineer appropriate solutions for varying requirements.

Systems Engineer—Network Modeling

Develop and maintain telephony, paging traffic, and capacity models for worldwide communications network.

Radio Frequency Systems Engineer

Design, develop, and test satellite-based communications systems for data, video, and audio; perform satellite interference and RFI analysis; conduct satellite link analysis; perform site surveys; and develop systems integration documentation for field implementation.

Communications Systems Engineer

Perform various assignments in the following areas: messaging protocols; digital communications systems design (including DSP design, RF modem performance measurement, and testing); real-time software applications; and feedback control systems.

Network Technicians

Conducts testing of network design. Maintains technical expertise in all areas of network and computer hardware and software interconnection and interfacing, such as routers, multiplexers, firewalls, hubs, bridges, gateways, etc. Evaluates and reports on new communications technologies to enhance capabilities of the network.

Satellite Communications Systems Engineer

Participates in the design, analysis, and test verification of the payload/communications subsystems of new and on-going satellite programs. Specific responsibilities include (1) perform communications subsystem design and analysis; support test and verification of the RF subsystem, including data review and trending; (2) develop RF/communications payload specifications and flow requirements from system/spacecraft/communication subsystem specs to all affected RF component, antenna and bus subsystems; (3) interface with suppliers and internal design teams to provide cost effective and low risk solutions; and (4) develop payload design documentation to communicate payload designs to internal design and business teams, vendors, and customers.

SatCom Engineer

The satellite modem development team will interface with system engineers and the board level hardware development and embedded software teams to work through systems issues and integrate these terminals for different applications from ground mobile to aeronautical, to fixed ground terminals. The ideal candidate should have a broad depth and knowledge in the areas of link budgets, RF technology, and digital communications theory.

Network Operations Center Technician

Use remote monitoring tools to identify issues with the satellite network or with customer equipment. He or she will then work with engineering to identify problems, investigate causes and recommend solutions. This role is the first line of communication with our clients and field staff; will be responsible for seeing the full resolution of trouble tickets

---

DATA SERVICES
REMOTE SENSING—UNDERSTANDING EARTH FROM ABOVE

Next to telecommunications, one application that is showing rapid growth is the use of remotely sensed data. From their vantage point high above the Earth, space-based sensors scanning Earth are providing users on the ground with an unprecedented array of information. With customers in the agricultural, mining, and oil exploration industries, to name a few, the potential number of users for this data is enormous.

Multi-spectral sensors onboard Earth-observing spacecraft produce data helpful in monitoring yields from global wheat production, tracking oil pollutants on the oceans, keeping an eye on river flooding, identifying locales of valuable minerals, and watching urban and rural growth patterns. As an example, the annual plotting of snow cover in the western United States can cost one-half million dollars to process the data, but it saves nearly $100 million annually in hydroelectric and irrigation efficiencies.

In the past decade dozens of new satellites have been launched into space that focus their sensors, cameras, or radar imaging systems toward the Earth, dramatically increasing the amount and type of data that is available and the need for data interpretation.

Revenues from Earth monitoring are on the increase and a new generation of users armed with this information can improve and better utilize the resources on our planet.

In the private sector, for example, DigitalGlobe offers data in resolutions, once the domain of classified intelligence agencies. Google Maps and Google Earth have become a staple of consumers. And entrepreneurial startups, such as Planet Labs, from its base in San Francisco, build and operate a network of satellites called "Doves." In January 2014, it delivered into space "Flock 1," a constellation of imaging satellites made up of 28 Doves. With subsequent launches, 81 Doves are now in space with the goal of imaging the entire Earth, every day.

The availability of cheap, high-powered computing systems combined with the expansion of data is enabling a new generations of users. As colleges and universities from around the world integrate remote-sensing analysis and usage courses into their programs in forestry, oceanography, farming, civil planning, and even archaeology, remote-sensing data is increasingly becoming integrated into everyday jobs, much as the computer, the Internet, and email have been assimilated into the workplace.

Jobs in This Area

Remote sensing is simply the ability to collect information from a distant location. Using satellites that contain sensors that are able to provide information about Earth, users on the ground are able to analyze this data for a variety of purposes.

In general, remote-sensing organizations perform at least one of following types of activities:

- Develop the systems and sensors that will collect the data
- Software to analyze the data
- Software or reports that will convey the data in an understandable format
- Research and analysis of the data for Earth monitoring, intelligence gathering, or geographical information systems (GIS)

Once the data is collected and relayed to the ground, the task of understanding the data is set to begin. Using graphical software packages, analysts are able to combine different data sets to generate a picture that will interest the end user. For instance, in order to assist a civil planner in locating the best site for a new facility, the following data sets might need to be combined:

- A digital terrain model showing the height and slope of the ground
- A population distribution model
- A data set showing roads and power lines
- Data showing underground streams

Analysts interpreting remotely sensed data have always been in high demand. With the development of automated software allowing the data to be more easily processed as well as the increase of data being derived from the sensors, the number of these positions is anticipated to increase over the next decade.

New software applications and analysis products are enabling the remote-sensing industry to target customers not normally associated with the space industry—farmers, architects and regional planners, geologists, and even archaeologists.

In general, many positions within the industry are involved with:

- Data interpretation and analysis
- Development of graphic interfaces
- Computer simulations
- Computer programming

These positions can be found in all three space communities— commercial, civil, and military—and include the analysis of data gathered for military intelligence, environmental monitoring and prediction, and weather monitoring and prediction.

Sample Classified Ads and Position Descriptions for
Remote Sensing and Photogrammetry

Imagery & Geospatial Analysts and Engineers

These positions are involved with software engineering; imagery analysis and exploitation; imagery tasking, collection and dissemination; geospatial/mapping analysis; cartography; photogrammetry; hydrography and communications; image processing; and multi- and hyperspectral imagery requirements and training.

Sensor Designers

Requires scientists and engineers with experience in any or all of the following: optics, RF and microwave design, and electronics.

Software Engineers—Graphical Information Systems

Mid-sized image handling systems to include image exploitation, image database applications and simulations. Will work with non-technical experts to develop accurate simulations using customer application software.

Senior Analyst

Position involves experience with digital photogrammetric workstations, stereo imagery control, and feature analysis.

Remote Sensing Team Leader

Ability to program and handle operating systems and natural resources data in a GIS environment.

Photogrammetrists and Technicians

Experience in aerotriangulation, CAD, digital orthophoto, stereo compilation, and systems management.

Imagery Analyst

Will exploit imagery and geospatial data from satellite and airborne systems in support of military operations. Plan and recommend the use of imaging sensors for reconnaissance and surveillance missions. Produce intelligence by studying and exploiting imagery to include visible, infrared and radar, both fixed and moving target indicator (MTI) and geospatial data.

DATA SERVICES:
GPS—NAVIGATING THE EARTH

The GPS is an all-weather, continuous operation, space-based radio navigation system that evolved from the first navigation satellites orbited in the early 1960s by the U.S. Navy to increase the target accuracy of submarine-launched missiles.

The satellite system, also known as Global Positioning System, consists of 38 satellites, which circle Earth twice a day and fly in a medium Earth orbit at approximately 12,550 miles altitude. Providing military and civilian users with worldwide position, velocity, and time information data, GPS is the most widely used system in the world for positioning and navigation products; although other satellite networks exist or are under development in Russia, Europe, China, and India.

GPS prevalence wasn't predicted at its start, and it was not always a commodity utilized by more than three billion users on a daily basis. From smartphones and mapping software to coordinating aviation traffic in the skies and precision farming, the past two decades have seen its commercial evolution from handheld devices that provided directional and emergency assistance to backpackers, hikers, and boaters to fully integrated electronic devices that are at the core to many electronic devices and systems. As the world becomes more digital, new systems are being developed that enable people to better track and coordinate everything from ships and cargo containers to lost pets. The need for electrical engineers and technicians, as well as software engineers, continues to remain strong in this multibillion dollar sector.

SCIENCE AND RESEARCH
MICROGRAVITY—MADE IN SPACE

Both commercial as well as government firms are looking at harnessing space for manufacturing "made-in-space" products. The exotic nature of space—specifically its microgravity environment—appears to be of benefit in making semiconductor materials, higher strength alloys, even pharmaceuticals. By reducing the forces of gravity on industrial processes, a diverse menu of products is hoped for. Research already conducted in space is pointing the way to such possibilities—products that are purer or exhibit qualities of greater value over their Earth-made counterparts.

Most recently, the introduction of 3D printing onboard the *International Space Station* shows great promise. A Zero-G Technology Demonstration (3D Printing in Zero-G) experiment demonstrated that a 3D printer works normally in space. In general, a 3D printer extrudes streams of heated plastic, metal, or other material, building layer on top of layer to create three-dimensional objects. Testing a 3D printer using relatively low-temperature plastic feedstock on the *International Space Station* is viewed as the first step toward establishing an on-demand machine shop in space, a critical enabling component for deep-space crewed missions and in-space manufacturing.

Making the most of microgravity means removing the gravity factor during formation of materials. Experiments conducted in orbit show that manipulating temperature, composition, and fluid flow can be controlled far better when the factor of gravity is removed.

A drawback to such experimentation, however, remains the high cost of access to orbit. Expensive space transportation costs are focusing commercial attention on low-volume, low-weight, and high-value products, such as pharmaceuticals, electronic components, optical devices, and metal alloys.

Research activities are expected to expand as opportunities for getting "time in space" increase—making use of the *International Space Station* and free-flying platforms or via parabolic aircraft flights. Several small firms, such as Nanoracks, identify and arrange opportunities for researchers and help them negotiate the paperwork associated with using NASA platforms.

As these opportunities expand, numerous products of commercial value are anticipated. A sample of these include:

- **Electronic Materials:** Pure, nearly perfect crystals are required in computers and numerous optical and electronic devices. Crystals, made of silicon or other material, are the basis for semiconductors, infrared sensors, and lasers. Space processing permits crystal purity and uniformity far beyond those possible on Earth.

- **Metals, Glasses, and Ceramics:** High-strength metals and temperature-resistant glasses and ceramics are essential to power generation, propulsion, aviation, aerospace, and related applications. Containerless processing in space permits the mixing and solidification of metals and ceramics in forms and at levels of purity that cannot be attained on Earth.

- **Biological Materials:** Separation of macro-molecules (proteins, enzymes, cells, and cell components) is fundamental to all fields of biological research. Collagen fibers, to replace injured human connective tissues, and urokinase—a drug for countering blood clots—are two biological substances that can be produced in space. Many more candidate pharmaceuticals have been tagged as suitable for manufacturing in microgravity, with greater efficiency, lower cost, and in greater purity levels than can be achieved on Earth.

Jobs in This Area

The use of the microgravity environment for research is a nascent commercial market that is expected to grow significantly in the future. Most microgravity research is currently performed within the government or academic communities. Hardware is developed at both government and commercial organizations. Opportunities exist within firms for:

- Designing and developing experiment hardware.
- Analyzing data derived from the experiments.
- Marketing microgravity hardware and facilities to potential users and researchers.
- Researching how microgravity affects processes that are well known on Earth. The mixing and properties of materials, fluid flow, and crystal growth, all function much differently in a microgravity environment.

Researchers within the academic and research community generally have a specialty background in areas such as molecular biology, biochemistry, cell-to-cell interaction, crystallography, or materials.

SCIENCE AND RESEARCH
SPACE SCIENCE AND ASTROPHYSICS

Almost all these positions are research oriented and are located at universities or at government-research facilities.

- **Space Sciences**—Includes positions engaged in the study and investigation of atmospheres and space phenomena, the heavenly bodies and their characteristics, astrophysics, and celestial mechanics. The following specializations are included in this group: aeronomy, ionosphere, fields and particles, stellar studies, lunar and planetary studies, meteoroid studies, solar studies. College majors for the above include physics, astronomy, meteorology, geology, geophysics, astrophysics, or other appropriate fields of basic physical science. Courses of interest include electronics, optics, materials, vibration, high-vacuum theory, heat transfer, and aerospace instrumentation.

- **Astrophysics**—The primary aim of the astrophysicist is to understand the physical processes governing the behavior of the atmospheres and space environments of Earth, Sun, and other planetary bodies. It includes research on the Earth's thermosphere, ionosphere, and magnetosphere as well as the solar wind and coupling among these regions. Other areas where astrophysicists get involved include activities related to galactic events, cosmic rays, solar wind, background radiation, pulsar research, black hole accretion, globular clusters, and the detection of new stars, galaxies, and planets.

- **Astrobiology**—Theoretical and experimental research on the nature and origin of life in the universe. Involves studies directed toward understanding the nature and basic mechanics involved with the synthesis of biologically significant compounds, the evolution and adaptation of life forms, and the development of life detection systems and devices suitable for space flights and exploration. Specialties include chemical evolution, biological adaptation, and life-detection systems.

SCIENCE AND RESEARCH
MEDICAL AND BIOTECHNOLOGY

- **Medical Research**—What is the impact of gravity on life and living systems? How does the human body adapt in space? What can we learn about space travelers that could be applied to conditions on Earth? (i.e., solving the problem of bone marrow loss by astronauts might lead to a cure for osteoporosis.)

- **Life Sciences**—Theoretical and experimental research on the effects of space environmental stresses upon living organisms and systems. Specialties include biochemical processes, psychological studies, plant studies, physiological studies, molecular biodynamics, radiobiological studies, and neurobiology.

- **Human-Machine Systems**—Theoretical and experimental research on the effects of space environment stresses upon man functioning as an integral component of a human-machine system for flight and exploration. Specialties include physiology, human performance studies, environmental control, manned systems engineering, and bionics studies.

Business and Administrative Positions

Numerous professional careers that do not require degrees in engineering and science are available in the space industry. Some of these are positions responsible for the following:

Marketing and Sales	Finance
Policy Analysis	Insurance
Management Consulting	Accounting
Publishing	Contract Administration
Proposal Coordinator	Business Analysts

Procurement	Human Resources
Public Affairs	Technical Writing and Editing
Legal & Licensing	Government Relations
Advertising Sales	Customer Service manager

Sample Classified Ads and Position Descriptions

Management Consulting

Assist companies in identifying market opportunities and developing strategies for competing in today's marketplace.

Program Management

Positions involve the technical and management direction of programs or projects. Incumbents prepare technical plans, budget and cost estimates, determine resources required for projects, and schedule phases of the work.

Business Development

Identify new business opportunities, coordinate opportunity evaluation and bid decisions, provide interface with customers, identify new markets for products.

Technical Writer

Write and edit sections for proposals, coordinate proposal tasks, verify compliance with specifications, and proofread corporate literature.

Proposal Coordinator

Duties include developing and executing proposal production and coordination plans, establishing and maintaining libraries of resumes, request for proposals, and submitted proposals. Familiarity with Word and Excel software is required.

Contracts Specialist and Procurement

Create, modify, and execute purchase orders, subcontracts and independent consultant agreements. Monitor agreements to assure that technical requirements are being met in a timely manner, in accordance with contract/agreement requirements; analyze cost proposals; and determine suitability of the cost breakdown, applicability of overhead rates, propriety of fee requested, and compliance with statutes regarding limitations.

International Relations
Coordinate international activities and partnerships for policy interactions, negotiate cooperative agreements, manage export activities, and participate in global marketing and sales activities.

Policy and Plans
Research and analyze issues. Provide in-depth information for government officials, industry leaders, specialists, journalists, etc.

Insurance
Perform risk analysis on satellites, launch vehicles, and operations.

Legal and Legislative Affairs
Attorney positions serve in a variety of roles similar to the non-space industry: contracts, labor law, patent and trademarks, as well as legislative affairs.

Colleges and Universities

In this chapter:

We will review the following topics in this chapter:

- Undergraduate and graduate educational programs and classes
- Finding student research activities
- Funding your education through space scholarship and fellowship opportunities
- Education that starts at the undergrad level and continues throughout your career.

"The greatest gain from space travel consists in the extension of our knowledge. In a hundred years this newly won knowledge will pay huge and unexpected dividends."

—Wernher von Braun
Pioneering rocketeer

GETTING STARTED: UNIVERSITY PROGRAMS

Choosing a college for your undergraduate or graduate studies can be a time-consuming and agonizing task. In addition to balancing location, course offerings, school reputation, professors' backgrounds, and financial aspects, you have also chosen the option of trying to find a school that will allow you to pursue a career in the space industry. Keep in mind that a space career does not necessitate a specific discipline or even that you participate in space-related programs while gaining your education.

Take, for instance, a technical career. Many engineers and scientists in the industry have a degree(s) in any one of the following: electrical engineering (circuits, control systems, etc.); mechanical engineering (structures, propulsion, fluid mechanics, etc.); materials and materials engineering (composite materials, ceramics, high-temperature metals, etc.); physics, chemical engineering, software and computer science engineering; robotics; etc.

Opportunities within the space industry are as broad as the degrees you may pursue—from engineering and science to business and management, policy analysis, and sales. The space industry has a position for almost anyone.

Even if you choose a school that does not have a major program or research effort in space, chances are that there are at least one or two professors with a similar interest or a small research study involved with disciplines that can be applied to space.

- Your time at a university is meant for you to gain a broad, diversified education.
- Your time in industry will be spent applying that knowledge.

Choosing an Area of Study

In choosing an undergraduate program, we recommend that you treat your education as a broader opportunity rather than focus on one specific school because it performs space research. Attending a school with a specific program may give you a clearer understanding of a specific part of the industry, but as an undergraduate, establishing a broad background may be more important in the long run. Keep in mind that a large number of people change or modify their career paths as time goes on. What you think you want to do today, may not be what you want to do tomorrow.

EXAMPLES OF SPACE-RELATED COURSES

(Titles taken from course catalogs of institutions mentioned later in this chapter.)

TECHNICAL COURSES

Space Vehicle Design

Earth System Science

Asteroids, Meteors, Comets

Observational Astronomy

Combustion Systems

Life Support Systems

Human Factors in Space

Celestial Mechanics

Theory of Propulsion

Satellite Propagation Effects

Aerospace Vehicles

Space Science and Exploration

Introduction to Orbital Mechanics

Satellite Information Processing

Computer Vision

Introduction Spaceflight Dynamics

Global Change

Technical Issues in Space

Quasars and Cosmology

Communications Theory

Deep Space Communications

Facilities Operations

BUSINESS AND POLICY

Strategic Implications of Space

Space Treaties and Legislation

Remote Sensing Policy and Law

Communications Policy

Strategic Planning

Space Policy and International Implications

China/Russian Space Program

Engineering Economics

Intro to Space Technology

Strategic Implications of Space

Fundamentals of Marketing

Universities with Space-Related Programs

There are a number of universities that offer degrees or specialized programs related to space. The list below has been compiled only to show the breadth of programs and activities available. It is not meant to provide a complete list of programs. You will find—at the end of this chapter—a more in-depth list of schools, along with information on how to contact them.

UCLA	Astronautical Engineering		McGill University	Space Law
Texas A&M	Space Power		George Mason	Geosciences Information
Carnegie Mellon	Robotics		Boston University	Center for Remote Sensing
University of Alabama Huntsville	Microgravity		MIT	Programs in Planetary Science
George Washington	Space Policy		Princeton University	Astronomy

A number of universities you may find have even launched their own student-built miniature satellites. To name but a few: Stanford, San Jose State, Cal Poly, University of Michigan, Brown, Iowa State, Utah State, and Montana State.

FINDING SPACE ACTIVITIES AT A UNIVERSITY WITHOUT A DEVOTED CURRICULUM

Don't worry if your university doesn't offer a degree program in aerospace engineering, there are plenty of other degrees that the industry finds valuable. To guide you on your path, you will have to do some research but more than likely you will be able to identify professors at your university who can suggest courses that your might want to take. A perfect example is R.P.I. (Rensselaer Polytechnic Institute) located in upstate New York, near the Vermont and Massachusetts borders. During the 1980s, while one of the book's authors attended, the school did not have a specific program or easily identifiable course offerings devoted to space or space sciences. When an inquiry was made to the mechanical engineering department faculty mentor, I was informed there were no classes in this area, but I could look at the aeronautical engineering courses. However, after investigating further, several programs and activities were identified: The university president at the time was George M. Low, a former deputy administrator of NASA; a professor with a research grant studying how space-based lasers could be used for Earth-to-orbit propulsion systems; and a number of research projects being funded by NASA in the areas of microgravity materials processing and robotic systems.

The lesson to be learned is that many universities can provide you opportunities to feed your interests, you just have to look closely and do some research.

GRADUATE DEGREE PROGRAMS

A graduate degree is meant to focus your early career in a given direction—either by emphasizing a more narrow specialization or by adding a discipline to your desired goal (MBA, in addition to a B.S. in Engineering). Two of the most important considerations in choosing a graduate program are your advisor and your research project. As with undergraduate activities, even schools without a narrow degree program may have a professor who can provide the opportunity for you to do research in a specific area. The U.S. government offers hundreds of millions of dollars in research grants to professors and schools throughout the nation. In addition, private industry sponsors numerous research endeavors. To find the graduate program and professor you want, you will need to undertake a research effort to determine your options. You may choose to make this task as simple as asking your undergraduate advisor to suggest a list of programs to investigate or as complicated as calling all potential universities and inquiring with whom to talk.

Before calling schools, unless you know exactly where you want to go, it is highly recommended that you talk with some people in the industry who are working in the specific area or field that you are hoping to pursue. It is more than likely that they may be able to tell you of an opportunity that you may not find otherwise.

There are many ways to find expert advice. The most direct way would be to ask your alumni relations department, your undergraduate department chairman, or even alumni at your fraternity/sorority. Contacts are everywhere; you only need to ask.

A list of some university programs placing an emphasis on space can be found at the end of this chapter.

FINANCING YOUR EDUCATION: SCHOLARSHIPS AND FELLOWSHIPS

Many of the space-related fellowships and scholarships that exist are offered by industry associations, NASA, or other government agencies. When looking for financing, it is recommended that you investigate all sources including the industry associations mentioned in Chapter 8. A number of fellowships and scholarships are listed below:

Scholarships and Grants

American Institute for Aeronautics and Astronautics Scholarships

http://www.aiaa.org

Scholarship Name	Unique Criteria	Sponsor	Value
Vicki and George Muellner Scholarship for Aerospace Engineering	Students studying a field to enter the aeronautics industry	Vicki and George Muellner	$5,000
Catherine and David Thompson Space Technology Scholarship	Students studying a field to enter the space industry	Catherine and David Thompson	$5,000
Liquid Propulsion Scholarship	NA	AIAA Liquid Propulsion Technical Committee	$2,500
Cary Spitzer Digital Avionics Scholarship	NA	AIAA Digital Avionics Technical Committee	$1,500
Ellis F. Hitt Digital Avionics Scholarship	NA	AIAA Digital Avionics Technical Committee	$1,500
Dr. Amy R. Pritchett Digital Avionics Scholarship	NA	AIAA Digital Avionics Technical Committee	$1,500
Dr. James Rankin Digital Avionics Scholarship	NA	AIAA Digital Avionics Technical Committee	$1,500
Space Transportation Scholarship	NA	AIAA Space Transportation Technical Committee	$1,500
Leatrice Gregory Pendray Scholarship	Female applicants only	AIAA Foundation	$1,250
Orville and Wilbur Wright Graduate	Graduate level researchers	AIAA Foundation	$5,000

Awards (multiple awards)			
Guidance, Navigation, and Control Graduate Award	Researching a guidance, navigation, and control topic.	AIAA Guidance, Navigation, and Control Technical Committee	$2,500
Martin Summerfield Propellants and Combustion Graduate Award	Researching a research topic related to propellants and/or combustion.	AIAA Propellants and Combustion Technical Committee	$1,250
Gordon C. Oates Air Breathing Propulsion Graduate Award	Researching an air breathing propulsion topic	AIAA Air Breathing Propulsion Technical Committee	$1,000
John Leland Atwood Graduate Award	NA	AIAA Foundation	$1,000

American Meteorological Society (AMS) Freshman Undergraduate Scholarship

The scholarship is open to all high school students and designed to encourage study in the atmospheric and related sciences.

http://www.ametsoc.org/amsstudentinfo/scholfeldocs/freshundergradscholarhip.html

AMS Graduate Fellowships

A $24,000 stipend is presented to each fellowship recipient for a nine-month period in the upcoming academic year.

http://www2.ametsoc.org/ams/index.cfm/information-for/students/ams-scholarships-and-fellowships/ams-graduate-fellowships/

ASPRS Awards Program

Offers 14 awards totaling more than $50,000 in value. Available to both undergraduate and graduate student-members of ASPRS and others, these resources have been generated with the intention of advancing academic and professional goals within the fields of photogrammetry, remote sensing, and related disciplines.

http://www.asprs.org/ASPRS-Awards-and-Scholarships.html

Award	Eligibility	Type of Grant	Grant Amount	Expectations
Altenhofen	Undergraduate or Graduate Students	One Year Award	$2,000	Report of scholastic accomplishments
Anson*	Undergraduates USA Only	One Year Award	$2,000	Final Report
Behrens*	Undergraduates USA Only	One Year Award	$2,000	Geospatial science or technology or land info systems
Colwell*	Doctoral Students USA or Canada	One Year Award	$6,500	Remote Sensing or related GIS
Fischer	Current or Prospective Graduate Student	One Year Award	$2,000	Final Report
DigitalGlobe	Undergraduate or Graduate Student USA or Canada	High-Res Digital Imagery	$20,000 potential value	Proposal and a report to selection committee
Moffitt*	Graduate or Undergraduate Students	One Year Award	$6,500	Final Report
Osborn*	Undergraduate Students; USA Only	One Year Award	$2,000	Final Report
Ta Liang	Current Graduate Student	Travel Grant	$2,000	Report to ASPRS and to Ta Liang's family
Wolf	Prospective Teachers/Graduate Students; USA	One Year Award	$4,000	Final Report

	only			
Z/I Imaging	Current or Prospective Graduate Student	One Year Award	$2,000	Final Report

Astronaut Scholarship Foundation (ASF)

More than 100 astronauts from the Mercury, Gemini, Apollo, Skylab, and Space Shuttle programs have joined in the mission to award merit-based scholarships to the best and brightest university students who excel in science, technology, engineering, and mathematics. Since its inception, ASF has awarded over $4 million in scholarships to more than 370 of the nation's top scholars via $10,000 awards. http://astronautscholarship.org

Dr. Robert H. Goddard Memorial Scholarship

The National Space Club awards a $10,000 scholarship each year, in memory of Dr. Robert H. Goddard, America's rocket pioneer. The scholarship is presented at the Goddard Memorial Dinner each spring, for the following academic year. The award is given to stimulate the interest of talented students in the opportunity to advance scientific knowledge through space research and exploration. http://www.spaceclub.org/education/goddard.html

Lady Mamie Ngan Memorial Scholarship

The American Astronautical Society offers $10,000 for students to attend the International Space University's Master of Science in Space Studies program conducted at the ISU Central Campus in Strasbourg, France, or at its regional summer program www.astronautical.org

The National Space Grant College and Fellowship Project

The project contributes to the nation's science enterprise by funding research, education, and public service projects through a national network of 52 university-based space grant consortia. The consortia fund graduate fellowships and undergraduate scholarships for students pursuing careers in science, mathematics, engineering and technology, or STEM, as well as curriculum enhancement and faculty development.
http://www.nasa.gov/education/spacegrant

NASA MUREP Funding

MUREP scholarship funds are competitive opportunities that focus on minority serving institutions and the underserved and underrepresented students in the science, technology, engineering, and math disciplines. The scholarship includes up to a $9,000 academic scholarship, not to exceed 75 percent of verified tuition, and $6,000 stipend for a required summer ten-week internship at NASA. http://www.nasa.gov/offices/education/programs/national/murep/home/index.ht ml#.VVqF1VLZmPI

NASA OE Scholarships

NASA OE Scholarships are a competitive yearlong opportunity focused on students in eligible NASA science, technology, engineering, and math (STEM) disciplines. Eligible students include rising freshman, sophomores, and juniors, at the undergraduate level, who will complete their undergraduate degree in spring 2016 or later and community college students, with at least two years remaining at the community college. The goal is to address the agency's mission-specific workforce needs. The scholarship includes up to a $9,000 academic scholarship, not to exceed 75 percent of verified tuition, and $6,000 for a required summer ten-week internship at a NASA center. https://intern.nasa.gov/ossi/web/public/main/

Sacknoff Prize for Space History

Annual prize to a university student consisting of trophy, $300 cash prize, publication in the peer-reviewed journal *Quest*, and the opportunity to present at the Society for the History of Technology annual meeting. http://www.spacehistory101.com/prize

Small Satellite Scholarship Program

Offered annually at the AIAA-Utah State University Small Satellite Conference for the student with the best application/research technology project that would benefit the small satellite industry. Multiple scholarships ranging from $2,500 to $10,000. http://www.smallsat.org

The Society of Satellite Professionals International (SSPI)

The SSPI Scholarship Program assists deserving high school and university graduates with meeting the high costs of undergraduate and post-graduate study in satellite-related disciplines. Through the generosity of scholarship sponsors, SSPI provides scholarships ranging from $2,500 to $3,500 to high school

seniors, undergraduate, and graduate students from locations around the world.
http://www.sspi.org

The USRA Scholarship Awards

Provides college scholarship awards to students who have shown a career interest in science or engineering with an emphasis on space research or space science education. Several $2,000, one-time awards are given.
http://www.usra.edu/about/outreach/scholarship/

Postdoctoral Opportunities

AFOSR Resident Research Associateship Program

Awards are made to doctoral-level scientists and engineers who can apply their special knowledge and research talents to research areas that are of interest to them and to the Air Force laboratories and centers. Awards are made to postdoctoral associates (within five years of the doctorate) and senior associates (normally five years or more beyond the doctorate). Each awardee works in collaboration with a research advisor who is a staff member of the research laboratory.
http://www.wpafb.af.mil/library/factsheets/factsheet.asp?id=9378

Einstein Postdoctoral Fellowship

Awards Fellowships to recent PhDs in astronomy, physics, and related disciplines. Einstein fellows hold their appointments at a host institution in the United States for research that is broadly related to the science goals of the NASA Physics of the Cosmos program. The proposed research may be observational, instrumental, theoretical, archival, or study sources from these missions at other wavelengths. The fellowship duration is three years (subject to review after the second year and to availability of funds from NASA).
http://cxc.harvard.edu/fellows/

Fellowships for Early Career Researchers

To facilitate the integration of new planetary science researchers into the established research funding programs and to provide tools and experience useful when searching for a more advanced (i.e., tenure-track, civil servant, or equivalent) position. Selected fellows have the opportunity to apply directly to the Early Career Fellowship program for up to $100,000 in start-up funds when they obtain a tenure-track or equivalent position. Participation is limited to proposers submitting research proposals to planetary science research programs http://nspires.nasaprs.com/external/solicitations/summary.do?method=init&solI d=%7B874EB6B2-2F61-C82D-B2D4-EE48CD9EB574%7D&path=open

The Hubble Postdoctoral Fellowship Program

Supports outstanding postdoctoral scientists whose research is broadly related to NASA cosmic origins scientific goals as addressed by any of the missions in that program. The research supported may be theoretical, observational, or instrumental. The fellowships are tenable at U.S. host institutions of the fellows' choice, subject to a maximum of one new fellow per host institution per year. The duration of the fellowship is up to three years: an initial one-year appointment and two annual renewals contingent on satisfactory performance and availability of NASA funds.
http://www.stsci.edu/institute/smo/fellowships/hubble

NAI Postdoctoral Fellowship Program:

Provides opportunities for PhD scientists and engineers of unusual promise and ability to perform research on problems largely of their own choosing, yet compatible with the research interests of NASA and the member teams of the NASA Astrobiology Institute. Note that the NAI does not participate in every application/award cycle, so check the ORAU post-doc page for details.
https://astrobiology.nasa.gov/nai/funding/nasa-astrobiology-postdoctoral-fellowship-program/

The NASA Postdoctoral Program (NPP)

One-to three-year, post-doctoral fellowships for highly talented national and international individuals to engage in research at NASA centers, or at a NASA-affiliated research institution. There are also opportunities via this program to perform science administration work at NASA Headquarters. Although primarily for recent doctoral graduates, "senior" NPP fellowships can also be awarded to researchers who have been active in their fields for a substantial amount of time. http://nasa.orau.org/postdoc/

National Air and Space Museum

Offers a variety of fellowships for predoctoral, postdoctoral, and non-academic researchers. http://airandspace.si.edu/research/fellowships/

- **Guggenheim Fellowships** are competitive three- to twelve-month in-residence fellowships for pre- or postdoctoral research in aviation and space history. An annual stipend of $30,000 for predoctoral candidates and $45,000 for postdoctoral candidates will be awarded http://airandspace.si.edu/research/fellowships/guggenheim.cfm

- **Verville Fellowship** is a competitive nine- to twelve-month in-residence fellowship intended for the analysis of major trends, developments, and accomplishments in the history of aviation or space studies An annual stipend of $55,000 will be awarded for a 12-month fellowship http://airandspace.si.edu/research/fellowships/verville.cfm

- **Charles A. Lindbergh Chair in Aerospace History** is a competitive twelve-month fellowship open to senior scholars with distinguished records of publication who are at work on, or anticipate being at work on, books in aerospace history. Support is available for replacement of salary and benefits up to a maximum of $100,000 a year. http://airandspace.si.edu/research/fellowships/lindbergh.cfm

- **Postdoctoral Earth and Planetary Sciences Fellowship** to support scientific research in this area. Scientists in the Center for Earth and Planetary Studies concentrate on geologic and geophysical research on Earth and other terrestrial planets, using remote-sensing data obtained from Earth-orbiting and interplanetary spacecraft. Research also focuses on global environmental change. Appointments can be made for one or more years. Stipends are compatible with NRC postdoctoral fellowships in the applicant's field. http://airandspace.si.edu/research/fellowships/ceps.cfm

National Space Biomedical Research Institute Postdoctoral Fellowship

NASA has an annual call that can be found at http://solicitation.nasaprs.com/open by searching for NSBRI.

Naval Research Lab Postdoctoral Fellowship

NRL sponsors a postdoctoral fellowship program at a number of Navy R&D centers and laboratories. The program is designed to significantly increase the involvement of creative and highly trained scientists and engineers from academia and industry to scientific and technical areas of interest and relevance to the Navy. https://nrl.asee.org/

Roman Technology Fellowship in Astrophysics

Provides early career researchers the opportunity to develop the skills necessary to lead astrophysics flight instruments/projects and become principal investigators of future astrophysics missions; to develop innovative technologies that have the potential to enable major scientific breakthroughs; and to foster new talent by putting early-career instrument builders on a trajectory toward long-term positions. The fellowship duration is one to five years (subject to a peer review process and availability of funds from NASA). http://science.nasa.gov/researchers/sara/student-programs/nancy-grace-roman-technology-fellowships-astrophysics-early-career-researchers/

Sagan Fellowship Program

Supports outstanding recent postdoctoral scientists to conduct independent research that is broadly related to the science goals of the NASA exoplanet exploration area. The primary goal of missions within this program is to discover and characterize planetary systems and Earth-like planets around nearby stars. Fellowship recipients receive financial support to conduct research at a host institution in the United States for a period of up to three years (subject to annual review and availability of funds from NASA). http://nexsci.caltech.edu/sagan/fellowship.shtml

Zonta International Amelia Earhart Fellowship

Established in 1938 in honor of famed pilot and Zontian Amelia Earhart, the fellowship is awarded annually to women pursuing PhD/doctoral degrees in aerospace-related sciences or aerospace-related engineering. The fellowship of $10,000, awarded to 35 fellows around the globe each year, may be used at any university or college offering accredited post-graduate courses and degrees in these fields.

http://www.zonta.org/WhatWeDo/InternationalPrograms/AmeliaEarhartFellowship.aspx

---

ENHANCING YOUR EDUCATION—
GETTING EXPERIENCE TO INCREASE YOUR EMPLOYMENT PROSPECTS

Regardless of what your major is, you can increase your chances of being offered a position and improve your resume by participating in research projects or by going on a cooperative education (COOP) assignment at a private company, participating in an on-campus research activity, and/or taking part in one of the many specialized programs sponsored by government agencies, such as NASA.

Companies place great emphasis on practical knowledge as compared to book knowledge. The ability to work with a team, knowing how to handle problems that arise on a project, and the ability to organize the tasks needed to finish a project, are skills that are better learned by doing than in a classroom.

COOPERATIVE EDUCATION PROGRAMS

COOP affords undergraduate students the opportunity to take a six-month to one-year leave of absence from school to work at a private or public institution and gain real-world experience. These programs are usually coordinated by employees of the career services and professional development office at your university. It is their role to arrange for employers to interview on campus. If you decide to pursue the COOP option and would like to find an assignment with a space focus, it is recommended that you do some research on your own. Many of the larger space companies offer COOP programs. As it is highly unlikely that they will all visit your campus for interviews, you should plan to contact them on your own or with the help of your COOP office.

ON-CAMPUS RESEARCH ACTIVITIES

Another option for gaining real-world project experience is through supporting a professor's sponsored research project. Although most research opportunities are reserved for graduate students, many professors save a few slots for undergraduates. While larger schools, or those with extensive research budgets, will inevitably have more opportunities, there will also be more competition for the prime activities.

Other opportunities exist at universities that house major non-profit research facilities. Several such examples are the Charles Stark Draper Laboratory with MIT; the Applied Physics Laboratory at Johns Hopkins University; the Space Dynamics Laboratory at Utah State University; and the Institute for Earth, Oceans, and Space at the University of New Hampshire.

Students should also talk with individual professors to see if they have a need for support.

High School Student Programs

Virginia Aerospace Science and Technology Scholars (VASTS)

A ten-week distance-learning program for Virginia high school juniors. The course consists of NASA-based, STEM-related curricula. The culmination of the online coursework is a six-day residential summer academy at NASA Langley Research Center. http://www.vasts.spacegrant.org/

Summer Programs

NASA Academies

The NASA Academy is a unique summer experience at the university level for developing future leaders of the U.S. Space Program. The program is an intensive, resident, 10ten-week summer experience with laboratory research work, a group project, lectures, meetings with experts and administrators, visits to NASA centers and space-related industries, technical writing, and presentations. Rising junior, senior undergraduate or at the early graduate level in accredited U.S. college or university as of May of the program year. Must be U.S. citizen or permanent resident (as of May of the program year).
https://www.nasa.gov/offices/education/programs/descriptions/NASA_Academy.html#.VVqIO1LZmPI

Planetary Science Summer School

This program seeks people who have a keen interest in planetary exploration, and who have completed their graduate work in science or engineering, to engage in an intensive one-week team exercise designed to teach the process of developing a robotic mission.
https://pscischool.jpl.nasa.gov/index.cfm

International Space University

The International Space University provides graduate-level training to the future leaders of the emerging global space community at its central campus in Strasbourg, France, and at summer session locations around the world.
http://www.isunet.edu/

The Air Force Research Laboratory (AFRL) Scholars Program

Offers stipend-paid summer internship opportunities to undergraduate and graduate-level university students pursuing STEM degrees, as well as upper-level high school students; select locations also offer internships to university students pursuing education-related degrees and K–12 professional educators. The selected interns gain valuable hands-on experiences working with full-time AFRL scientists and engineers on cutting-edge research and technology and are able to contribute to unique, research-based projects. Graduate interns are able to collaborate with AFRL on current research and incorporate the research into their graduate work.
http://afrlscholars.usra.edu/overview/

Summer Fellowship Program at the Center for Space Nuclear Research

Undergraduate and graduate level students experience cutting-edge research in nuclear power and propulsion technologies at the Center for Advanced Energy Studies. As a CSNR summer fellow, you work as part of a team of students and with scientists at the Idaho National Laboratory (INL) to complete a research project of current interest to NASA in potential nuclear technology performance. The summer fellows program allows participants to experience a real research environment, to learn from top-notch nuclear scientists, and to preview careers in research.
http://csnr.usra.edu/public/default.cfm?content=322

Undergraduate Research Opportunities

NASA's Planetary Geology and Geophysics
Undergraduate Research Program

Undergraduates majoring in geology or related fields take part in an eight-week summer internship program, in which qualified students get to work with a NASA-funded planetary scientist at the scientist's home institution. In the past, sites have included NASA Ames Research Center, NASA's Jet Propulsion Laboratory, the U.S.G.S. Astrogeology Branch in Flagstaff, Arizona, and many others. http://www.acsu.buffalo.edu/~tgregg/pggurp_homepage.html

NASA Undergraduate Student Research Program (USRP)

Offers undergraduates across the United States mentored internship experiences at NASA centers and research support facilities. Currently sponsored through the NASA Office of Education, this program is analogous in many ways to the NESSF program sponsored by the Science Mission Directorate. http://www.epo.usra.edu/usrp/

Summer Research Experience for Undergraduates (REU) Program

A competitively selected program designed to support current sophomore and junior undergraduate students to work with scientists at the SETI Institute and at the nearby NASA Ames Research Center on projects spanning the field of astrobiology from microbiology to observational astronomy.
http://www.seti.org/reu/

The Lunar and Planetary Science Summer Intern Program

Undergraduates with at least 50 semester hours of credit to experience cutting-edge research working one-on-one with a scientist at the LPI or at the NASA Johnson Space Center on a research project of current interest in lunar and planetary science.
http://www.lpi.usra.edu/lpiintern/

Graduate Opportunities

NASA Earth and Space Science Fellowship (NESSF) Program

Supports graduate students in basic and applied research in Earth science and space science. Awards of $30,000 per year are made for up to three years. Information and application instructions can be found at http://solicitation.nasaprs.com/open by searching for NESSF.

NASA Graduate Student Researchers Program

The project offers competitive fellowships to U.S. citizens who are pursuing graduate degrees at the master and doctoral levels, at U.S. accredited colleges and universities in areas of science and engineering that support the NASA research and development mission. GSRP and other NASA Office of Education fellowship opportunities can be found via the NASA One Stop Shopping Initiative (OSSI) online application system at: http://intern.nasa.gov

NASA Harriett G. Jenkins Predoctoral Fellowship Project (JPFP)

This and other NASA Office of Education fellowship opportunities can be found via the NASA One Stop Shopping Initiative (OSSI) online application system at: http://intern.nasa.gov

NASA Space Technology Research Fellowships (NSTRF)

Open to U.S. citizens or permanent resident students who have applied to, been admitted to, or are already enrolled in, a full-time master's or doctoral degree program at accredited U.S. universities. Information and application instructions can be found at: http://solicitation.nasaprs.com/open by searching for NSTRF.

The National Consortium for Graduate Degrees for Minorities in Engineering and Science, Inc., Fellowship

GEM assists underrepresented minority students in obtaining MS degrees in engineering and PhD degrees in engineering and the natural and physical sciences. http://www.gemfellowship.org/

Department of Defense (DoD) National Defense Science and Engineering Graduate Fellow Program (NDSEG)

The NDSEG fellowship program is a joint program of the United States Army, Navy, and Air Force within the University Research Initiative (URI), designed to increase the number of U.S. citizens trained in science and engineering disciplines important to defense goals. http://www.onr.navy.mil/en/Education-Outreach/undergraduate-graduate/NDSEG-graduate-fellowship.aspx

Accredited Aerospace Degree Programs

(Courtesy: Council of Higher Education Accreditation)

Astronautical Engineering

Capitol College	Laurel, Maryland	http://www.captechu.edu/academics/undergraduate-academics/bachelor-degree-programs/astronautical-engineering
Naval Postgraduate School	Monterey, California	http://www.nps.edu/Academics/Schools/GSEAS/Departments/SpaceSystems/index.html
Purdue University	West Lafayette, Indiana	https://engineering.purdue.edu/AAE

Ohio State University	Columbus, Ohio	https://mae.osu.edu/aeronautical-and-astronautical-engineering-program
UCLA	Los Angeles, California	http://www.mae.ucla.edu
University of Washington	Seattle, Washington	https://www.aa.washington.edu/

Aerospace Engineering

Air Force Institute of Technology	Wright-Patterson AFB, Ohio	http://www.afit.edu
Arizona State	Tempe, Arizona	http://semte.engineering.asu.edu/aerospace-engineering/
Auburn University	Auburn, Alabama	http://www.eng.auburn.edu/aero/
Cal Poly, San Luis Obispo	San Luis Obispo, California	https://aero.calpoly.edu/
Cal Poly, Pomona	Pomona, California	https://www.cpp.edu/~aro/
Cal State, Long Beach	Long Beach, California	http://web.csulb.edu/colleges/coe/mae/
Case Western Reserve	Cleveland, Ohio	http://engineering.case.edu/emae/
Embry Riddle	Daytona Beach, Florida	http://www.erau.edu/
Embry Riddle- Prescott	Prescott, Arizona	http://prescott.erau.edu/
Florida Institute of Technology	Melbourne, Florida	http://coe.fit.edu/mae/
Georgia Tech	Atlanta, Georgia	http://www.ae.gatech.edu

Illinois Institute of Technology	Chicago, Illinois	http://engineering.iit.edu/mmae
Iowa State University	Ames, Iowa	http://www.aere.iastate.edu/
MIT	Cambridge, Massachusetts	http://aeroastro.mit.edu/
Mississippi State University	Mississippi State, Mississippi	http://www.ae.msstate.edu/
Missouri University of Science	Rolla, Missouri	http://mae.mst.edu/
New Mexico State	Las Cruces, New Mexico	http://mae.nmsu.edu/
NC State University	Raleigh, North Carolina	http://www.mae.ncsu.edu/
Oklahoma State	Stillwater, Oklahoma	http://www.mae.okstate.edu/content/aerospace-osu
Penn State University	University Park, Pennsylvania	http://www.aero.psu.edu/
Princeton University	Princeton, New Jersey	http://www.princeton.edu/mae/
St. Louis University	St. Louis, Missouri	http://parks.slu.edu/departments/aerospace-mechanical-engineering/
San Jose State	San Jose, California	https://ae.sjsu.edu/
San Diego State	San Diego, California	http://aerospace.sdsu.edu/aerospaceengineering/
SUNY Buffalo	Buffalo, New York	http://www.mae.buffalo.edu/
Syracuse University	Syracuse, New York	http://eng-cs.syr.edu/our-departments/mechanical-and-aerospace-engineering/

Texas A&M	College Station, Texas	http://engineering.tamu.edu/aerospace
University of Alabama	Tuscaloosa, Alabama	http://aem.eng.ua.edu/
University of Alabama, Huntsville	Huntsville, Alabama	http://www.uah.edu/eng/departments/mae/
University of Kansas	Lawrence, Kansas	http://ae.engr.ku.edu/
Tuskegee University	Tuskegee, Alabama	http://www.tuskegee.edu/academics/colleges/ceps/aerospace_science.aspx
USAF Academy	Colorado Springs, Colorado	http://www.usafa.edu/df/dfan/aero/aero_major.cfm
US Naval Academy	Annapolis, Maryland	http://www.usna.edu/AeroDept/
University of Arizona	Tucson, Arizona	http://ame.arizona.edu/
UC Davis	Davis, California	http://mae.ucdavis.edu/
UC Irvine	Irvine, California	http://mae.eng.uci.edu/
UC Los Angeles	Los Angeles, California	http://www.mae.ucla.edu/
UC San Diego	La Jolla, California	http://maeweb.ucsd.edu/
University of Central Florida	Orlando, Florida	http://mae.ucf.edu/
University of Cincinnati	Cincinnati, Ohio	http://ceas.uc.edu/aerospace.html
UC Boulder	Boulder, Colorado	http://www.colorado.edu/aerospace/
University of Florida	Gainesville, Florida	http://www.mae.ufl.edu/

University of Illinois at Urbana	Urbana, Illinois	http://aerospace.illinois.edu/
University of Maryland	College Park, Maryland	http://www.aero.umd.edu/
University of Miami	Coral Gables, Florida	http://www.mae.miami.edu/aerospace_engineering.php
University of Michigan	Ann Arbor, Michigan	http://www.engin.umich.edu/aero
University of Notre Dame	Notre Dame, Indiana	http://ame.nd.edu/
University of Oklahoma	Norman, Oklahoma	http://www.ou.edu/coe/ame.html
University of Tennessee	Knoxville, Tennessee	http://mabe.utk.edu/
University of Texas	Arlington, Texas	http://www.ae.utexas.edu/
University of Virginia	Charlottesville Virginia	http://www.mae.virginia.edu/NewMAE/curriculum/resources-for-undergraduates/
University of Washington	Seattle, Washington	https://www.aa.washington.edu/
Virginia Polytechnic Institute	Blacksburg, Virginia	http://www.aoe.vt.edu/
West Virginia University	Morgantown, West Virginia	http://www.mae.statler.wvu.edu/
Wichita State	Wichita, Kansas	http://www.wichita.edu/ae
Worchester Polytechnic Institute	Worchester, Massachusetts	http://www.wpi.edu/academics/aero.html

Aeronautical Engineering

Clarkson	Potsdam, New York	http://www.clarkson.edu/mae/
Daniel Webster College	Nashua, New Hampshire	http://www.dwc.edu/academics/ programs/engineering/undergrad /bs_ae.cfm
Rensselaer Polytechnic Institute	Troy, New York	http://mane.rpi.edu/
Western Michigan	Kalamazoo, Michigan	http://wmich.edu/mae/

* * *

Remote Sensing Programs

Arizona State University	Remote Sensing and Spatial Analysis	http://more.engineering.asu.ed u/windlab/?page_id=24
Boston University	Center for Remote Sensing	http://www.bu.edu/remotesens ing/
Cornell University	School of Civil and Environmental	http://www.cee.cornell.edu/
Florida International University	GIS Center	http://gis.fiu.edu/
George Mason University	Earth System and Geoinfo Science	https://cos.gmu.edu/about/rese arch/#centers
Georgia Tech	School Earth and Atmospheric Sciences	http://www.eas.gatech.edu/
MIT	Earth, Atmosphere, and Planetary Sciences	http://eapsweb.mit.edu/
Naval Postgraduate School	Remote Sensing Center	http://www.nps.edu/rsc/
Purdue University	Lab for Applications of Remote Sensing	http://www.lars.purdue.edu/

Texas A&M	GIS Science and Remote Sensing	http://geography.tamu.edu/research/giscience-and-remote-sensing
University of Arizona	Remote Sensing and Spatial Analysis	http://ag.arizona.edu/oals/rssa/rssa.html
University of California Davis	Spatial Technologies and Remote Sensing	http://www.cstars.ucdavis.edu/
University of Colorado at Boulder	Remote Sensing	http://www.colorado.edu/catalog/2012-13/content/remote-sensing
University of Miami	Remote Sensing Group	http://yyy.rsmas.miami.edu/groups/rrsl/
University of Michigan	Geosciences and Remote Sensing	http://aoss.engin.umich.edu/pages/graduate/grs http://wwweb.eecs.umich.edu/RADLAB/content/remote-sensing
University of Minnesota	Remote Sensing and Geospatial Analysis Lab	http://rsl.gis.umn.edu/
University of New Hampshire	Institute for Study of Earth, Oceans, and Space	http://www.eos.unh.edu/
University of Rhode Island	Laboratory for Terrestrial Remote Sensing	http://www.ltrs.uri.edu/
Washington University	Remote Sensing and Geospatial Analysis	http://depts.washington.edu/rsgal/
Western Michigan University	Earth Sciences Remote Sensing	http://www.esrs.wmich.edu/
Yale University	Center for Earth Observation	http://yceo.yale.edu/

Other Programs

American Military University (online)	Space Studies	http://www.amu.apus.edu/academic/programs/list
American Public University (online)	Space Studies	http://www.apu.apus.edu/lp2/space-studies
International Space University	Space Studies	http://www.isunet.edu
McGill University, Montreal	Institute of Air and Space Law	http://www.mcgill.ca/iasl/institute-air-and-space-law
MIT	Man Vehicle Laboratory	http://mvl.mit.edu/
MIT	Space Nanotechnology Lab	http://snl.mit.edu/
MIT	Space Systems Lab	http://ssl.mit.edu/newsite/
Rice University	Masters in Space Studies	http://www.profms.rice.edu/spacestudies.aspx?id=1003
Stanford University	Aeronautics and Astronautics	http://aa.stanford.edu/
University of Maryland	Space Systems Laboratory	http://ssl.umd.edu/
University of Maryland	Space Power and Propulsion Lab	http://www.sppl.umd.edu/
University of Mississippi	Remote Sensing, Air, and Space Law	http://www.spacelaw.olemiss.edu/
University of North Dakota	Department of Space Studies	http://www.space.edu/
UCLA	Earth, Planetary, and Space Sciences	http://epss.ucla.edu/
University of Texas at Austin	Center for Space Research	http://www.csr.utexas.edu/rs/

* * *

Top Graduate Schools for Astronomy
(Courtesy: *2014 U.S. News and World Report*)

California Institute of Technology	Pasadena, California	http://www.astro.caltech.edu/
Columbia University	New York, New York	http://www.astro.columbia.edu/
Cornell University	Cornell, New York	http://astro.cornell.edu/
Harvard University	Cambridge, Massachusetts	http://astronomy.fas.harvard.edu/
Johns Hopkins University	Baltimore, Maryland	http://physics-astronomy.jhu.edu/
MIT	Cambridge, Massachusetts	http://web.mit.edu/astronomy/
Pennsylvania State University	University Park, Pennsylvania	http://astro.psu.edu/
Princeton University	Princeton, New Jersey	http://www.princeton.edu/astro/
Stanford University	Stanford, California	http://web.stanford.edu/dept/astro/
UC Berkeley	Berkeley, California	http://astro.berkeley.edu/
UC Santa Barbara	Santa Barbara, California	http://web.physics.ucsb.edu/~astrogroup/
University of Chicago	Chicago, Illinois	http://astro.uchicago.edu/
University of Maryland	College Park, Maryland	http://www.astro.umd.edu/
University of Texas	Austin, Texas	http://www.as.utexas.edu/
University of Wisconsin	Milwaukee, Wisconsin	http://www.astro.wisc.edu/
Yale University	New Haven, Connecticut	http://astronomy.yale.edu/

A more in-depth list of schools offering astronomy programs can be found in Appendix C.

Other Sources of Education

Your education doesn't end with college. Sometimes it is
necessary to keep up-to-date with the latest technologies or a job
change to a new field makes it necessary.

Advancing Your Career

- Determine your training needs and develop an education
  plan.
- Clarify how you'd like to gain new skills.

1–5 Day Training Courses

- Many are sponsored by associations or take place at
  conferences, so visit the later sections of this book to
  identify target groups and visit their website calendars.

- There are also a number of non-affiliated groups that offer
  training. One that offers a number of space-related courses
  is the Applied Technology Institute www.aticourses.com.

FINDING A JOB FOR THE FIRST TIME...
OR THE NOT SO FIRST TIME

The next three chapters take you through what are perhaps the most valuable lessons you can learn in your professional career:

- Identifying the opportunities and the resources that can assist your job hunting efforts
- Learning the value of networking and where to do it
- Taking the next step...words of wisdom from an industry executive on how to make a firm **want** to hire you.

"Your work is going to fill a large part of your life, and the only way
to be truly satisfied is to do what you believe is great work.
And the only way to do great work is to love what you do.
If you haven't found it yet, keep looking. Don't settle.

—Steve Jobs
Apple Corporation

SPACE—JUST LIKE ANY OTHER INDUSTRY

After completing your search for employment in the space industry, you will realize that the resources and knowledge you uncovered during your search are similar to those used when searching for employment in other industries—classified advertisements, industry publications, the Internet, etc.

Similarly, industry recruiters will give the same kind of advice to those considering employment in this business that they would to others.

- Today's global economy stresses flexibility, the ability to adapt skills to different tasks. Employees who can handle a wide range of tasks will be in higher demand.

- Keep in mind that even when companies downsize or reduce staff, many are still hiring to fill needs.

- Small and mid-size companies have historically grown faster than large companies and do much of the hiring in an industry.

- It is usually easier to transfer from within a company than to get the exact position you want when first applying.

- If you're on the outside of the industry looking in, it may not be as difficult as it appears to obtain a position within the space industry. Although the retail and space industries would appear to have little in common, an employee from the retail industry could bring in needed knowledge in distribution and marketing.

- Traits such as communication skills and the ability to work well in a group are highly desirable.

Step One: Identify Target Organizations

You've started to take the first step to getting a solid foundation on the industry by reading this book, but the space industry has a wide range of opportunities. After you begin to narrow your choices on what type of job you are interested in—for example, rocket engineering vs. telecommunications marketing vs. environmental monitoring—your next step is to identify companies, but more so, you should focus your initial research on:

√   What is the makeup of the company or organization (do you prefer big or small)?
√   Is it in R&D mode or does it market products and services?
√   Is it an established company, an entrepreneurial startup, or government organization?
√   What specific products/missions is it working on?

To find information, use the following:

√   Company websites: Explore the site to gain a better understanding
√
√   Online Search: Type in the name of an organization or a project. You'd be amazed what can be online.
√   Survey Media Coverage: Can be a valuable source to identify current activities and names of key personnel.
√   LinkedIn (and competitors): Search for the company, review what is written (it'll be a short synopsis), and make note of any people you know or contacts that you'd like to make. Make note of employees who went to the same university, previously worked at the same company, etc.

Step Two: Identifying Where the Jobs Are

When searching for publicized opportunities, there are several places to look:

- √   Industry Trade Publications
- √   University Career and Professional Development Centers
- √   Industry Associations
- √   Internet and Print Classified Advertisements

PUBLICATIONS

Trade publications and those targeting industry "enthusiasts" can be a valuable source of information to give you a better understand of the topics, trends, and programs that have people talking.

While classified advertising in the industry's trade publications have historically been limited, publications such as *Space News, Via Satellite, Aviation Week and Space Technology,* and *Aerospace America,* do contain a handful of job openings. The titles of other industry publications can be found by going to your public library and asking the reference librarian for *Gale's Directory of Publications* or by reviewing an industry directory, such as the *International Satellite Directory* or the *Satellite Industry Directory.*

Local papers in cities with a heavy industry concentration, such as the *Washington Post,* the *Los Angeles Times, Florida Today,* and the *Houston Chronicle,* usually contain more ads than the industry publications. A search in a recent high-technology supplement of the *Washington Post* revealed more than 100 space-related job descriptions from around the United States.

Trade Newspapers and Magazines

Space News 1414 Prince Street, Suite 300 Alexandria, VA 22314 Tel: +1 (571) 421-2300 info@SpaceNews.com www.spacenews.com	*Via Satellite* 4 Choke Cherry Rd, Rockville, MD 20850 Tel: +1 (301) 354-2000 http://www.accessintel.com/
Aviation Week 1911 North Fort Myer Drive, Suite 600, Arlington, VA 22209 Tel: +1 (800) 525-5003 Tel: +1 (847) 763-9147 www.aviationweek.com	*Aerospace America (AIAA)* 1801 Alexander Bell Drive, Suite 500 Reston, VA 20191-4344 Tel: +1 (703) 264-7500 http://www.aerospaceamerica.org/

For the Enthusiast

Air and Space Smithsonian Institution PO Box 37012 MRC 513 Washington, DC 20013-7012 Tel: 2026336070 http://www.airspacemag.com/ist/?next=/	*Ad Astra* National Space Society 1155 15th Street NW, STE 500 Washington, DC 20005-2725 Tel: (202) 429-1600 nsshq@nss.org http://www.nss.org/adastra/
Quest: The History of Spaceflight PO Box 5752 Bethesda, MD 20824-5752 http://www.spacehistory101.com	*Spaceflight* British Interplanetary Society London, United Kingdom http://www.bis-space.com/what-we-do/publications

Online Publications

www.space.com	www.universetoday.com
www.thespacereview.com	www.spaceref.com
www.spacepolicyonline.com	spacereport.blogspot.com
www.nasawatch.com	spacenews.com/thedownlink/
www.spaceflightnow.com	acuriousguy.blogspot.com

INDUSTRY ASSOCIATIONS

As part of their missions, most associations usually have a goal of educating members and the public. As part of this goal, many of them maintain a formal or informal mechanism for notifying members about open positions. Usually, the associations promote these in one of three ways: via advertisement in their member publication, via advertisement on their website, or via job fairs or posted job bulletins at their conferences.

With the diversity of skills needs and the activities and skills taking place within the space industry, a wide range of associations exist focusing on everything from specific technical disciplines to enthusiasts interested in promoting the exploration of space. Joining an association allows you to keep on top of the industry in your area of interest and provides you with the opportunity at conferences and meetings to network and meet others.

A list of associations and regular industry conferences can be found in Chapter 8: Networking.

INTERNET RESOURCES: GAINING A SOLID FOUNDATION ONLINE

The Internet is by far the best source for finding available positions and researching companies, with a vast array of resources to explore. Many companies, especially the larger ones, offer links from the main homepage to a database of open positions within the company. Additionally, many (but not all) are compiled by specialty sites devoted to employment opportunities. Some contain more information than others and many do not contain categories directly related to space employment. So you may have to be patient and type in a number of search terms beyond that of space, satellite, NASA, etc. So don't be discouraged if the first site you evaluate doesn't have any positions related to your keyword(s).

The employment sites with the largest number of unique monthly visitors (more than 20 million) are:

- Indeed.com   http://www.indeed.com
- Monster.com   http://www.monster.com
- Glassdoor.com   http://www.glassdoor.com
- Careerbuilder.com   http://www.careerbuilder.com

A few sites have categories or focus on the industry itself, such as:

- Space Careers   http://www.space-careers.com
- Space Job Center   http://www.spacejobcenter.com
- Matchtech   http://www.matchtech.com/aerospace-jobs/

Additionally, many of the large print newspapers, near NASA or defense facilities with industrial hubs focused on space, still generate significant revenues from classified advertisements. Among these worth searching are:

- *Houston Chronicle*   http://www.chron.com/jobs
- *Washington Post*   https://jobs.washingtonpost.com/
- *Los Angeles Times*   http://www.latimes.com/business/jobs/

UNIVERSITY CAREER AND PROFESSIONAL DEVELOPMENT CENTERS

University career services and professional development offices are another good source of job opportunities. While these offices are set up to help current students or graduates of the university, many allow limited use by the general public as a community service. Career services and professional development offices receive open position notices from many companies that have had success in the past hiring students or graduates from that university. In addition to announcing entry level positions, many firms will also submit announcements for more senior personnel.

Many colleges and university career centers, along with more than 5 million employers participate in the NACElink Network, an alliance including the National Association of Colleges and Employers. The network is a national recruiting network and suite of Web-based recruiting and career services tools focused on new graduates entering the workforce. The site allow on-campus usage without a password and off-campus usage with a password, the system contains all the job postings that private organizations want to announce to members of that universities' community. Each company specifies which universities it wants to have access to the specific announcements. One open position may be viewed only by Cornell and MIT, while another position may state Rensselaer Polytechnic Institute, Princeton, and the University of Maryland. Passwords and logon information can be received from the alumni or career services and professional development offices at each university.

Another site catering to the community of recent or future graduates is http://college.monster.com.

PUBLIC LIBRARIES

Don't forget a search at your public library. In addition to numerous books on writing résumés, interview skills, etc, the reference section of the library contains numerous publications and access to databases which are generally out of the financial reach of the average job seeker. Among these resources will be:

- Directories providing details on public, private, and non-profit organizations
- Information on the major employers in a given geographic area

OTHER RESOURCES

Appendix B contains a list of organizations to aid you in your search. With nearly 2,000 organizations operating in the sector, it is only a small piece of what is out there. We've tried to provide a list representing larger firms, institutions that are doing significant hiring, and some that we expect you'd be looking for.

Before writing to an organization, we recommend that you call first or visit their website to learn more about the organization and its specializations and capabilities and to identify the appropriate point of contact for recruiting/personnel matters.

* * *

OTHER OPTIONS

Keep in mind that, in addition to direct employment, there are other options you may want to consider—specifically, temporary or contract assignments or starting your own firm.

TEMPORARY AND CONTRACT EMPLOYMENT

If you are interested in evaluating an organization, evaluating an employment activity you are capable of performing but are unsure if you want a career in, or want to work short-term to see a different area of the world, you may want to investigate non-permanent employment. Also, if you are trying to work for a specific company that does not have a current opening, a temporary position can allow you to get your foot in the door. This approach allows companies to evaluate employees and their performances prior to hiring them on a permanent basis.

Contract employment positions are generally short-term assignments (three months to two years) for technical positions. These positions typically pay substantially better than direct employment, as they usually carry no benefits or any guarantee of having the contract extended for any period of time. It can also give you the opportunity to work overseas (more on this later). Needless to say, there is no job security as a contract employee.

Important note: Never work with a contract employment agency that asks for payment for their services. Reputable firms are paid by the organization looking for talent.

Additionally, many companies also make use of local temporary agencies to fill administrative, professional, or technical positions. Most of these agencies can be found in a search of your target area.

Remember: Although designed to be temporary, the job that you're hired to do could lead to a permanent position with the firm if those around you are satisfied with your performance. This is similar to some of the reasons why cooperative education (COOP) assignments and summer employment are important to finding future employment (as mentioned in Chapter 6 on Colleges and Universities).

Contract Employment Organizations and Publications

(with a focus on aerospace jobs)

CJ Hunter.com / Contract Employment Weekly

The CJHunter.com website and its print publication:

> *Contract Employment Weekly*
> C.E. Publications, Inc.
> P.O. Box 3006, Bothell, WA 98041-3006,
> Phone: +1 (425) 806-5200
> staff@cjhunter.com
> http://www.cjhunter.com/

Belcan Corporation

Belcan Corporation provides engineering, staffing, and other flexible workforce solutions to clients around the globe. https://belcantechnicalstaffing.com

Modis International

A market leading specialist in the provision of IT and engineering staffing, consultancy and business solutions. Delivers solutions to over 2,500 clients from offices in 60 locations. http://www.modis.co.uk/

CTS International

Finds and fills highly technical jobs www.ctsinternational.com

BEING YOUR OWN BOSS

Got a better way of doing something? Perhaps there is a technology that you developed or worked with and think is great, but no one at your organization wants to do anything commercial with it. There is something exciting about wanting to take control, be your own boss, and control your own destiny. And if you can change the world or challenge the status quo in the process, even better. Entrepreneurism is hot and new firms are being created by those who simply choose the option of stepping outside and setting up their own organization.

Many space industry ventures do not require billions of dollars to get off the ground. Office expenses for software and hardware have become so modest that it does not always require a vast sum to set up a business. Anyone with a computer and programming skills can create a computer or mobile app and bring it to market. Likewise, there are many people who offer public relations, marketing research, and consulting services because the cost and the effort to launch are manageable. If you're an entrepreneur and have some experience, perhaps starting your own company is the answer.

RESOURCES AVAILABLE TO START-UP ORGANIZATIONS

SBIR
The Small Business Innovation Research (SBIR) program is a federal program that was started as a means to ensure that small firms were able to get some of the vast amounts of research and development funding spent by the government. The SBIR competition was designed to set aside a pool of money for which only small companies could compete. Over time the program has grown to distribute almost $1 billion annually, given out by the eleven federal agencies. Among the agencies that have SBIR programs and space-related topics in their solicitations are NASA, the Department of Defense, and NOAA.

Companies that win (historically, about one in seven or eight) can receive up to $100,000 for a Phase I, six-month effort, which can be followed by a Phase II award of up to $750,000. Companies retain the non-government intellectual property rights for four years.

For solicitations listing the technical topics under this program, contact the Small Business Administration or any of the participating federal agencies.

SBA 7A LOAN GUARANTEE PROGRAM

The Small Business Administration offers guarantees of up to 80 percent on loans made by banks or lending institutions to small businesses. Those SBA-backed loans allow the financial institution to make riskier loans to new companies without a track record and without substantial collateral. Contact for this program is through your local bank or through the regional SBA Office (check your local listings). Not all banks participate or are familiar with the program, so you will need to inquire.

MENTOR PROGRAMS

Many university business schools have established programs that can provide an individual or a company with a mentor—someone who has worked in or who has retired from industry. These mentors usually have extensive experience and provide advice on a variety of business-related topics, usually at no or minimal charge. Even if your local college or university doesn't have a program, inquire whether anyone there is aware of someone who might be willing to assist you with advice.

OVERSEAS OPPORTUNITIES

While many in the United States would like to work overseas—in Europe perhaps—the opportunities outside the United States for an American citizen are limited—unless they have several years of technical experience in a needed discipline. To reduce unemployment, many countries have imposed strict rules and regulations that state how and when companies can hire someone from outside the country.

For instance, a French company must first offer the position to a French national and then to a member of the European community before it can be offered to a citizen of the United States.

Note that the United States has similar laws. Historically, however, it has been much easier for a foreign national to get a job in the United States than the other way around.

If you are determined to find employment opportunities overseas, we recommend trying these methods:

1. Working as an employee of a U.S.-based company assigned to an overseas office
2. Working with a contract employment agency that specializes in bringing in high-tech talent for short-term (usually up to two years) assignments
3. Contacting non-U.S. companies and government agencies directly to determine their needs and ask for their assistance
4. Searching the Internet

SPACE ORGANIZATIONS LOCATED OUTSIDE THE UNITED STATES

Though most positions usually go to citizens of the host nation, most of which are either government entities or funded by government entities, hiring of non-citizens is not unknown.

The following sites will provide you with information about a number of non-U.S. organizations and government agencies

The Americas

√   Brazil / National Institute for Space Research

http://www.inpe.br/ingles

√   Brazil / Agencia Espacial Brasileira   http://www.aeb.gov.br/

√   Canadian Space Agency   http://www.asc-csa.gc.ca/eng/

Europe

√   European Space Agency   http://www.esa.int

√   France / CNES   http://www.cnes.fr

√   Germany / DLR   http://www.dlr.de/dlr/en/

√   Italy / Italian Space Agency   http://www.asi.it

√   Russian Federal Space Agency   http://en.federalspace.ru/

√   UK Space Agency   https://www.gov.uk/government/
organisations/uk-space-agency

Asia

√   Japan / JAXA   http://global.jaxa.jp/

√   India/ Indian Space Research Organization

http://isro.gov.in

√   Korea / Korea Aerospace Research Institute

http://eng.kari.re.kr/

Mid-East

√   Israel Space Agency   http://most.gov.il/english/space/

NETWORKING: YOUR KEY TO SUCCESS

In this chapter

We explore how and why to network through organizations, symposia, and events for networking opportunities.

> "Skill is fine, and genius is splendid, but
> the right contacts are more valuable than either."
>
> —Sir Arthur Conan Doyle

Regardless of your current or future needs, networking is one of the most important activities for advancing your career. In many cases, it is not what you know, but whom you know, and it's whom you know that can give you information few have. Statistics show that classified ads make up only 10–15 percent of all available jobs.

A Networking Example

Prior to moving to Washington, DC, one of the authors met with an industry consultant. The consultant didn't know of any positions within his organization, but he suggested that I contact three other people he knew and said to mention that he referred me. One of those three suggested talking to a small company down the hall, which was expanding at the time. This led to a job offer.

To network effectively, think about who might be a good contact. Your list should include the following: family, friends, college professors, college alumni, present and former supervisors, people you've met at industry events, and people you've met at social events.

Keep in mind—

1. Contacts provide valuable information about existing or upcoming opportunities, which are never published.
2. A contact may not be helpful immediately, but may become valuable in the future. Example: A recent graduate met an insurance broker at a luncheon. Three years later, the broker started a venture capital fund and invested in an idea the former student had. Remember: You never know who will end up where.
3. A company recruiter is more likely to hire someone who comes with a recommendation from a current employee. Networking gives you contacts on the inside.

QUESTIONS TO ASK

You will need to tailor your questions according to the contact you are talking to—someone working in your area of interest, personnel manager, friend of the family, etc. However, the following questions are meant to help guide you in general for questions you may want answered.

- What does your company look for when hiring?
- What sort of positions is your company filling today or expect to be filling in the future?
- How easy/difficult is it for me to find employment in my area of interest?
- What knowledge and skills are the most important?
- How important is it for a person in a position of this type to have knowledge of the industry? (e.g., this would be more important for a job in public relations, media, legal, etc., than for the duties of a propulsion engineer.)
- What training and experience do you think would be valuable?
- How often do you feel bored or frustrated in your type of work?
- What do you do on a typical day?
- What sort of practical experience would be valuable? Knowledge of...?
- What previous jobs led to your position?
- Are there similar types of positions in the area that I am interested in?
- What are the required qualifications and training for an entry-level position?
- Can you recommend any courses to take?
- What related fields or studies do you suggest I explore?
- Do you have any special advice you can offer?

Most important, always ask as your last question...
I appreciate your time; is there anyone else who you suggest that I talk with?

In turn, expect that the people you talk with will ask you the following questions:
- Where did you get my name? (It's usually helpful to mention this in advance, as they may be more willing to meet with you, if they know who referred you.)
- Why did you get interested in the industry?
- What courses have you taken? What is your background?
- What are your short/long-term career goals?

PUT WHAT YOU'VE LEARNED IN A DATABASE

In order to keep track of the details of your networking experience, it is recommended that you take advantage of today's technology to keep notes on the following. Your records should prove useful as well as providing you with discipline for the future.

- Name and title of each person you contacted
- The company and address
- How did you find this person? Who referred you?
- The date of contact.
- Your method of contact—via telephone, letter, at a meeting
- The context of your discussion
- Any follow-up that is required

GROWING YOUR NETWORK ONLINE

Establishing a professional network online is a critical asset that you will rely on over time. Whether it's to keep track of colleagues as they change positions, reach out to them to learn of opportunities, or to identify new relationships, an online presence is as important to an individual as it is to a business. And while it only takes a little bit of time to set up a profile, managing it will take a bit more, but from a networking perspective it is worth it. It is an integral part to identifying colleagues and keeping in touch as they move throughout their, and your, career.

Still keep in mind that a professional profile needs to be conservatively managed. As the saying goes, "think before you post." As a professional, you need to always control your image because nothing on the Internet truly disappears. More and more companies are reviewing profiles of prospective applicants, whether LinkedIn, Facebook, or another site, to see what they've said about past employers and colleagues and to determine what level of professionalism they bring to the table.

Make use of LinkedIn Groups to connect with other alumni as well as to identify those working for a company you are interested in. Many of the larger organizations also post open positions on their LinkedIn page.

WHERE TO NETWORK

Now that you've determined what questions to ask and what information you seek, it is time to get involved and seek out people with similar interests. Much of the networking in an industry takes place at the following:

- Sessions at conferences and symposia
- Exhibitions at conferences
- Association events, including industry speakers, networking breakfasts and luncheons
- University alumni events

Conferences, Symposia, Exhibitions

Conferences and their exhibit areas are usually sponsored by industry publications, associations, or technical societies. If you don't have the money to attend, don't worry. You can usually gain admittance to the exhibit area for free or a nominal charge.

Walking around the exhibit floor is a highly valuable networking exercise. In fact, if your primary purpose is networking, rather than expanding your understanding of a subject being explained by a speaker or presenter, the exhibit floor is where you want to be. Instead of sitting in a "classroom," you are talking to people.

This does not mean you should avoid the sessions. If you are registered for the conference, and there is a speaker talking on the area in which you are interested in working, it is highly advised that you listen to the talk and approach the speaker after the session has ended. Session breaks are often the best opportunities to network.

IDENTIFYING NETWORKING OPPORTUNITIES
JOIN AN ASSOCIATION / ATTEND A CONFERENCE

The space industry is home to dozens of organizations—professional, technical, and social—which provide information and bring together like-minded individuals. With more than a hundred events of different sizes and located around the world, they provide an excellent chance to network; whether it is a technology, i.e., the AIAA Space Propulsion Conference or the AIAA Guidance, Navigation, and Control Conference; a focus point, i.e., The Hosted Payload and Smallsat Summit or the AAS International Space Station Research and Development Conference; or as part of a continuing education requirement, i.e., the American Bar Association's Forum on Air and Space Law.

The easiest way to identify these opportunities is to keep track of the professional organizations that best relate to your area of interest. Even if you are not a member, details for many of these events will appear on their websites. What follows are some of the larger associations and groups and the major industry exhibitions that draw the largest crowds.

Professional and Technical Associations

American Institute of Aeronautics and Astronautics
With more than 35,000 individual members and 100 corporate members, AIAA is the world's largest technical society dedicated to the global aerospace profession. It offers a number of scholarly journals, technical book series, an aerospace library, and a database containing more than two million abstracts, sponsors nearly two dozen technical meetings each year, and hosts nearly 100 technical and standards committees.

AIAA
1801 Alexander Bell Drive, Suite 500, Reston, VA 20191-4344
Tel: +1 (703) 264-7500
http://www.aiaa.org

American Astronautical Society

Founded in 1954, the AAS has long been recognized for the excellence of its national meetings, technical meetings, symposia, and publications and for their impact on shaping the U.S. space program. Members have opportunities to meet with leaders in their field and in related disciplines, exchange information and ideas, discuss career aspirations and expand their knowledge and expertise. Among its activities are the annual Goddard Symposium (Washington, DC), the von Braun Symposium (Huntsville, Alabama), and publication of the *Journal of Astronautical Sciences* and *Space Times* magazine.

> American Astronautical Society
> 6352 Rolling Mill Place, Suite 102, Springfield, VA 22152-2370
> Email: aas@astronautical.org
> Tel: +1 (703) 866-0020
> http://www.astronautical.org

International Astronautical Federation

The IAF is an international space advocacy organization based in Paris, France, and founded in 1951 to foster dialogue among scientists around the world and support international cooperation in all space-related activities. Its 270 members from 64 countries around the world are drawn from space agencies, industry, professional associations, government organizations and learned societies. It is linked with the International Academy of Astronautics (IAA) and the International Institute of Space Law (IISL) with whom the IAF organizes the annual International Astronautical Congress.

> IAF
> 94 bis, Avenue de Suffren, Paris France 75015
> Tel: +33 (1) 45.67.42.60
> http://www.iafastro.org/

Society of Satellite Professional International

SSPI promotes the growth of the satellite industry by educating the public and end users about the contributions of satellites and connecting satellite professionals worldwide through education, knowledge-sharing and fostering professional relations. In addition to an annual gala and awards ceremony held during the Satellite 'XX' conference in Washington, DC, the group hosts regional speakers and networking events sponsored by local chapters.

> SSPI International HQ
> 250 Park Avenue, 7th Floor, New York, NY 10177
> Tel: +1 (212) 809-5199
> http://www.sspi.org

American Society for Photogrammetry and Remote Sensing

Founded in 1934, the ASPRS is a scientific association serving over 7,000 professional members around the world. The mission is to advance knowledge and improve understanding of mapping sciences to promote the responsible applications of photogrammetry, remote sensing, geographic information systems (GIS), and supporting technologies.

> ASPRS
> 5410 Grosvenor Lane, Suite 210, Bethesda, MD 20814-2160
> Tel: +1 (301) 493-0290
> http://www.asprs.org

The National Space Club

Located in Washington, DC, with chapters in the National Space Club is a non-profit organization devoted to fostering excellence in space activity through interaction between industry and government, and through a continuing program of educational support. Awards are offered to recognize significant achievements in space science and enterprise. Scholarships and other education support are a major focus of club activity. It hosts the annual Goddard Memorial Dinner in Washington, DC, known as the "Space Prom."

National Space Club
204 E Street, NE Washington, DC 20002
Tel: +1 (202) 547-0060
http://www.spaceclub.org

Florida: http://www.nscfl.org
Huntsville: http://spaceclubhsv.org/

Public Interest Organizations

National Space Society

The National Space Society (NSS) is an independent, educational, grassroots, non-profit organization dedicated to the creation of a spacefaring civilization. Founded as the National Space Institute (1974) and L5 Society (1975), which merged to form NSS in 1987, NSS is widely acknowledged as the preeminent citizen's voice on space. NSS has over 50 chapters in the United States and around the world. The society also publishes *Ad Astra* magazine, an award-winning periodical chronicling the most important developments in space. Focused on exploration and development and the settlement of space.

National Space Society
1155 15th Street NW, Suite 500, Washington, DC 20005-2725
Tel: +1 (202) 429-1600
http://www.nss.org

A directory of local chapters throughout the world can be found at:
http://chapters.nss.org/a/lists/

The Planetary Society

The Planetary Society, founded in 1980 by Carl Sagan, Bruce Murray, and Louis Friedman, is a membership organization of individuals with a goal to inspire and involve the world's public in space exploration through advocacy, projects, and education. Areas of interest include searching for life in the universe, hunting for Earthlink planets, and scanning the skies for dangerous asteroids. Its flagship magazine is *The*

Planetary Report, which features articles and photos to provide comprehensive coverage of discoveries on Earth and other planets.

> The Planetary Society
> 85 South Grand Avenue, Pasadena, CA 91105
> Tel: +1 (626) 793-5100
> http://www.planetary.org

Space Frontier Foundation

Founded in 1988, the Space Frontier Foundation is an advocacy organization committed to realizing the vision of a greatly expanded and permanent human presence in space.

> Space Frontier Foundation
> 42354 Blacow Road, Fremont, CA 94538
> http://www.spacefrontier.org

Students for the Exploration and Development of Space (SEDS)

SEDS, typically located at a university, is a non-profit organization of passionate and driven students dedicated to expanding the role of human exploration and development of space.

> SEDS-USA
> 3840 East Robinson Rd PMB176, Amherst, NY 14228
> http://seds.org/

Industry Exhibitions

Among the hundreds of conferences, symposia, and events hosted by these and other space-related organizations, some draw the largest crowds.

National Space Symposium

Sponsored by the U.S. Space Foundation and held annually in the spring in Colorado Springs, Colorado, the policy-focused conference and exhibition feature a range of companies and organizations involved with the military, civil, and commercial space programs. The event draws a number of military officers involved locally with the U.S. Space Command, Air Force Space Command, Peterson Air Force Base, and the Air Force Academy.

Spacefoundation.org
425 Arrowswest Drive, Colorado Springs, CO 80907
Tel: +1 (719) 576-8000
www.spacesymposium.org

Satellite "XX"

Sponsored by the Satellite Group of Access Intelligence, the publisher of the industry trade journal, *Via Satellite*, the event is the premier event for satellite-enabled communications. The event offers technical sessions, symposia, and a exhibition area. Held in Washington, DC, usually in March, it attracts more than 12,000 visitors and a few hundred corporate exhibitors, which focus on satellite and component manufacturing and services related to the utilization of satellites for communications solutions and other applications.

Access Intelligence, LLC
4 Choke Cherry Road, Rockville, MD 20850
Tel: +1 (301) 354-2000
info@accessintel.com
www.satshow.com

SATCON

Held in New York City, the CCW+SATCON incorporates several important vertical markets under one roof with an expo that features the latest satellite, fiber, broadband, wireless, and hybrid network technologies for government, military, broadcasters, telecommunications, enterprise firms, IP Networking, mobile communications, and emergency response applications.

http://www.ccwexpo.com/satcon/

AIAA / Utah State University Conference on Small Satellites

Dedicated to the technical and business aspects of small satellites, the show draws more than 1,000 people, including many smaller organizations and universities.

http://www.smallsat.org/

Robert Goddard Memorial Symposium (Washington, DC)
von Braun Memorial Symposium (Huntsville, AL)

Two-day long space policy discussions, which are sponsored by the American Astronautical Society.

American Astronautical Society
6352 Rolling Mill Place, Suite 102, Springfield, VA 22152-2370
Tel: +1 (703) 866-0020
http://www.astronautical.org

International Space Development Conference

The annual conference of the National Space Society. The conference covers several broad areas of study related to building a spacefaring civilization, including transportation to and through space, technology needed to live and work in space, and Earth-based activities to advocate for or educate others about space development.

National Space Society
1155 15th Street NW, Suite 500 Washington, DC 20005-2725
Tel: +1 (202) 429-1600
http://isdc.nss.org

International Astronautical Congress

Drawing from its government, industrial, and academic users from around the world, this annual event, held in a different country and location each year, is the largest gathering of space professionals focused on human spaceflight, robotic spaceflight, exploration, and science.

9 4 bis, Avenue de Suffren, 75015 Paris France
Tel: +33 (1) 45 67 42 60
http://www.iafastro.org/

Other Professional Groups
Providing Networking Opportunities

Colorado Space Business Roundtable

Its mission is to promote the growth of space and space-related industry in Colorado.

> 9785 Maroon Cir, Suite 350, Englewood, CO 80112
> 4425 Arrowswest Dr. Colorado Springs, CO 80907
> Tel: +1 (720) 440-2088
> info@coloradosbr.org
> http://www.coloradosbr.org/

Commercial Spaceflight Federation

The Commercial Spaceflight Federation (CSF) is the industry association of leading businesses and organizations working to make commercial human spaceflight a reality.

> 500 New Jersey Avenue NW, Suite 400, Washington, DC 20001
> Tel: +1 (202) 715-2928
> http://www.commercialspaceflight.org

Future Space Leaders Foundation

The Future Space Leaders Foundation is dedicated to the advancement of career development opportunities for the next generation of space and satellite industry professionals.

> 5335 Wisconsin Avenue, NW; Suite 520, Washington, DC 20015
> Tel: +1 (202) 639-8845
> http://www.futurespaceleaders.org/

Maryland Space Business Roundtable

MSBR is an organization that encourages the growth and development of aerospace-related business in Maryland. Each month, the MSBR holds an event with guest speakers that represent a cross-section of top political, NASA, and DoD leaders.

3235 Atlee Ridge Rd, New Windsor, MD 21776
Tel: +1 (443) 340-4634
www.mdspace.org

Space Generation Advisory Council

SGAC works on the international, national and local level to link together university students and young professionals to think creatively about international space policy issues and inject the new generation point of view into international space policy creation.

info@spacegeneration.org
http://www.spacegen.org/index.php/en/

Space Transportation Association

Space Transportation Association is dedicated to supporting policies that advance robust, affordable space transportation for NASA, DOD, and commercial markets. The association's corporate members are launch manufacturers and launch service providers. STA Breakfast Series hosts speakers and a forum to chat about issues.

204 E Street NE, Washington, DC 20002
Tel: +1 (202) 547.0229
www.spacetransportation.us

Washington Space Business Roundtable

Its primary activity is a monthly luncheon, which brings together a broad range of executives, government policy makers, lawyers, insurers, analysts, academics, and thought leaders involved in the business of space in the metropolitan Washington region.

c/o Longbottom Communications, LLC
2343 N. Vernon Street, Arlington, VA 22207-4056
Tel: +1 (703) 528-5492
http://www.wsbr.org/about.html

Women in Aerospace (WIA)

WIA is dedicated to expanding women's opportunities for leadership and increasing their visibility in the aerospace community. The membership of women and men shares an interest in a broad spectrum of aerospace issues, including human spaceflight, aviation, remote sensing, satellite communications, robotic space exploration, and the policy issues surrounding these fields.

> 204 E Street NE, Washington, DC 20002
> Tel: +1 (202) 547-0229
> http://www.womeninaerospace.org/

Yuri's Night

Yuri's Night is a global celebration of humanity's past, present, and future in space. Yuri's Night parties and events are held around the world every April in commemoration of Yuri Gagarin becoming the first human to venture into space on April 12, 1961, and the inaugural launch of the first Space Shuttle on April 12, 1981.

> https://yurisnight.net/

WORKING IN THE SPACE INDUSTRY

Biography & Advice

Name	Charles Bolden Jr.
Organization	NASA
Job Title	Administrator
Location	Washington, DC

Degrees/School
BS, Electrical Science, U.S. Naval Academy
MS, Systems Management, University of Southern California

Career Highlights
- Retired U.S. Marine Corps Major General
- Marine aviator and test pilot, logging more than 6,000 hours of flight time
- Deputy Commandant of Midshipmen (US Naval Academy)
- Astronaut: STS-61C (pilot), STS-31 (pilot), STS-45 (mission commander), and
  STS-60 (mission commander)
- Administrator of NASA

Words of Wisdom*
Whatever field you will be entering through your studies...my advice for you is quite simple...dream big dreams; do what you want to do; don't listen to anyone who tells you can't do something or you don't belong; do your job and do it very well; and don't let the opportunity to make a difference in your world pass you by.

The writer Zora Neale Hurston said, "No matter how far a person can go, the horizon is still way beyond you." There's truly much to behold on the horizon, and all of you are at the leading edge of reaching for it, no matter what your field of expertise.

I'm a military man and an astronaut. But only one of those paths was on my radar when I was your age...I never dreamed of being an astronaut and flying in space and none of that would have occurred...had it not been for the mentorship and encouragement of a kind and generous man, the late Dr. Ron McNair, who challenged me to not be afraid of challenging myself—to believe what my mom and dad had told me for as long as I can remember—that I could do anything I wanted to do...But I would have to be willing to study hard and work hard to attain my goals—I would have to have faith in my ability and myself.

You'll realize that what you learned here [at the university level] is only the beginning of your story. Like my systems engineers always tell me, there is just nothing that can take the place of what you learn on the job.

* Excerpts from a commencement speech given at the University of Michigan, 2014

A Foot in the Door...Now What?

In this chapter

Words of wisdom are shared with you from an industry executive.

Great. You've identified an opportunity or a company you'd like to work for. You may even have an "in" at the firm after chatting with someone you met at an event or a conference. And this is where the fear for many people sets in, as they wonder how not to screw this up.

How do you write a good résumé? How do you interview? These are not topics that we plan to cover in any detail—there are hundreds of books written by experts on these subjects.

But before you head out there....here are some words of wisdom:

Three Reasons I'd Look Twice at Your Résumé

This section comes to you from Marillyn Hewson, the Chairman, President, and CEO of Lockheed Martin.

I've hired thousands of people over the course of my career, which means I've read tens of thousands of résumés. I've seen great résumés that have helped people launch thriving careers—and, unfortunately, I've seen plenty that have fallen flat.

A résumé is your first impression on a potential employer. And in many cases, it will determine whether you get the chance to make a second impression.

At Lockheed Martin, it's not unusual to get hundreds of applicants for a single job opening, so the competition is intense. It's important to take the time to make sure you stand out—and stay—in a potential employer's mind.

In my experience, a few simple steps can help take your résumé to the top of the pile.

1. Don't be afraid to delete

Your résumé is not an autobiography. In fact, less is more in crafting a good summary of your skills and experience. A tight résumé shows me that you can prioritize. It tells me that you can be clear, concise, and get right to the point.

It also shows me that you respect my time. Hiring managers—at any level of leadership—are busy. And the fact that they're hiring means they likely have even more work on their plate than usual.

Don't expect the hiring manager to weed through your résumé looking for experience that's relevant to the opening. Honestly assess whether every single word belongs. Odds are, you'll find places to trim—and that's a good thing.

2. Re-write your résumé for every job description

Don't just send the same résumé and cover letter to every job opening. Really pay attention to the job description, and make sure that your application underscores why you're perfect for that particular position.

Companies spend a lot of time and energy crafting job descriptions to attract the right candidates. So learn from them and use it to your advantage. Job postings are great input to help you understand what the organization really needs.

When you focus your résumé on the job description, and align your skills to the organization's needs, you're demonstrating that you understand exactly what they're looking for. And you can better show how you are the right person for the job.

3. Show me results

Use your résumé as an opportunity to showcase all your hard work. I don't just want to see a list of previous positions and responsibilities—I want to see the results you delivered.

Did you increase sales? Did you land a big contract? Did you complete a project under budget? Did you improve customer satisfaction or employee engagement? Each of these examples is a real, tangible accomplishment—and accomplishments say more about your experience than a long list of jobs you've held.

Specific examples show me that you are ready and able to help the organization succeed. So for each position you list, highlight the one or two achievements you are most proud of. Demonstrate how valuable you were, and how valuable you can be.

These three suggestions are important whether you're applying for a top management position or your first job out of school. They can help you make that first impression that will land you an opportunity to interview. And I have some suggestions for that, too.

Would I Hire You? My Top Five Interview Questions

When you are the Chairman, President, and CEO of Lockheed Martin, one of the largest aerospace and defense companies in the world, what do you, Marillyn Hewson, look for?

One of the most important things I do as a leader is choosing the people who will join our team. Finding the right person to lead a group, manage a project, or fill a key position is critical to the success of any organization.

And it's not easy.

Résumés are useful for showing the skills and qualifications of a candidate, but they don't tell the whole story. Effective interviews are the real key to understanding if someone has the strategic thinking, leadership skills, and collaborative approach that will deliver results.

When I interview prospective employees, I look for a proven track record and specific experiences that I believe indicate future success. At the same time, I also probe to see if the individual is aligned with our corporate values and will fit with our culture.

Here are the five interview questions I have found most useful—and what I look for in a candidate's answers:

1. How did you spend the first 90 days of your previous job?

The best employees are those who bring real energy and initiative to the job. I like to know whether you're the kind of person who can set priorities, take initiative, and drive results right from the beginning.

This is why I like to ask how you approached your last job. I'm looking for specific examples of how you got to understand the organization and integrate with the team. I want to hear about your early wins, accomplishments, and successes. Learning about how you tackled the early days of your last job gives me a good indication of how you will hit the ground running if you were to join my team.

2. What is the biggest challenge you've faced, and how did you handle it?

The actual challenge and solution aren't so important. I'm more interested in *how* you worked through the problem. Candidates need to demonstrate strategic thinking and strong problem-solving skills. And, just as important, they need to know when and how to ask for help.

Did you engage your teammates in implementing a solution? Did you work with your customer to make sure everyone was onboard? Did you keep your leadership informed early so there were no surprises? These answers tell me how you deal with issues, address problems, and manage stakeholders.

3. How would the people you've worked with describe you?

What would your boss, colleagues, and customers say if I asked them what it's like to work with you? Are you a team player or a lone operator? Are you a big picture person, or do you focus on the details? Do you have high standards of integrity, or do you bend the rules to get things done faster?

I'm looking for answers that demonstrate the leadership qualities and personal values that we seek in our top performers. At Lockheed Martin, we call this Full Spectrum Leadership and it consists of five imperatives:

1. We look for leaders who can shape the future by establishing goals and laying out a plan to achieve them.
2. We also want our people to build effective relationships, whether they're with colleagues, employees, or customers.
3. We want leaders who can energize the team, engaging and inspiring others to do their best work.
4. We need people who deliver results, understand our strategy, and meet their commitments.
5. And, most important, we want people who model personal excellence, integrity, and accountability in all they do.

These qualities are especially important at Lockheed Martin, though they should serve you well in almost any role. No matter what field you're in, it always pays to have a full spectrum leader on the team.

4. What is one area you'd like to improve, and what are you doing about it?

Of course, no one is perfect—and I would never hire someone who thinks that they are. Yet great employees go beyond simply being aware of their shortcomings, they are actively working on them. Are you working with a coach or mentor? Have you taken a public-speaking class? Do you engage in 360-degree feedback sessions? We all have things we'd like to work on, and I want to see that you have the drive to better yourself, grow professionally, and continue to learn.

5. Why should I hire you?

I like to end an interview with this simple question. The best candidates make a strong case for themselves. They can clearly articulate why they are the best choice for the job—and they can tell me what unique qualities they bring that no one else can offer. I want to see confidence in one's capabilities with awareness of one's opportunities for growth. This is no time to be shy; it's the time to be your own best advocate.

WORKING IN THE SPACE INDUSTRY

Biography & Advice

Name	Kobie Boykins
Organization	Jet Propulsion Laboratory
Job Title	Principal Mechanical Engineer
Location	Pasadena, CA

Degrees/School
B.S. Mechanical Engineering, Rensselaer Polytechnic Institute

Responsibilities
- Managing engineering managers
- Technical resource on mechanical actuators and motors and general spacecraft and instrument design
- Design and delivery of mechanical hardware

Career Path
I decided I wanted to be a space craft engineer in 5th grade. I wanted to be Geordi La Forge from *Star Trek*, he is the engineer. From there I started my trek to become a mechanical engineer so I could build the first interstellar vehicle. I chose RPI as it is a great engineering school with a relationship with NASA. I was offered an internship (COOP) at the Jet Propulsion Laboratory. From there I worked to get a job at JPL and have been there ever since.

Why Space?
I am a huge *Star Wars* and *Star Trek* fan and love the idea of being able to work on the cutting edge of technology. As I got older, working in the space industry opened up the ability to continue learning and being challenged everyday.

Words of Wisdom
NEVER STOP LEARNING. Failure is not an end, its a beginning. Learn from all your mistakes, and never make the same mistake twice. Find the thing you love to do, and do that everyday of your life. Boredom is an insult to oneself—this is not mine, but I really like it.

Astronaut: The Right Stuff

In this chapter

We explore knocking on NASA's door and private sector opportunities.

It has been said that for most, working in space "is a dream not a career."

While we realize that attaining astronaut status is a lifelong dream for many, becoming an astronaut is far more difficult than being picked for the National Basketball Association or the National Football League This fact is not meant to discourage, but it is reality. In future decades, we may all have the chance to travel into space. For now, opening up the space frontier remains the domain of a select cadre of people.

NASA's
Astronaut
Class of 2013

DREAMING OF SPACE

No doubt, many of you reading this book aspire to become 21st-century versions of "The Right Stuff." That was the expression coined by author Tom Wolfe in his book and movie of the same name. Wolfe's characterization of tough-as-nails experimental aircraft test pilots and the fearless set of America's first astronauts for the Mercury program created a persona that is still in evidence today.

But the astronaut corps has come a long way since the early 1960s when Alan Shepard was heralded as the first U.S. astronaut. He was shot skyward from Cape Canaveral, Florida, and landed in his Mercury capsule into the Atlantic Ocean on May 5, 1961, rocketing through air and space for all of 15 minutes. While historic, that suborbital trip pales in comparison to later space sojourns.

Today, nearly 55 years later, more than 535 people from some 38 nations have headed for orbit, the majority of them boosted there during the era of the U.S. Space Shuttle program. NASA has selected 20 groups of U.S. astronauts since the "Original Seven" in 1959. For numbers of U.S. astronauts—along with space travelers of other countries—they have take up semi-permanent residence in the *International Space Station.* Perhaps the dawning of single-stage-to-orbit rocketry may open up the prospect for commercial space pilots to fly between space and low Earth orbit (LEO), taking routes likely to be called the "LEO Run," for short.

But until commercial opportunities bring the price down from a $45–50 million per person per trip for an orbital visit to the *International Space Station* or $75,000–250,000 for a suborbital jaunt, the number of private space pilots will remain small and likely to be chosen from retired government or military astronaut corps. Until then, government remains the primary career path.

However, do keep an eye on such private space entrepreneurial efforts, such as Bigelow Aerospace of North Las Vegas, Nevada. It is in the business of providing expandable space habitats. It is looking to establish its own private astronaut corps. Beyond the Bigelow Aerospace industrial and scientific interests, Bigelow modules have the potential for becoming hardware for space tourism and missions destined for the Moon and Mars.

So before you lower your helmet visor to the locked position and get ready to ride a "mountain of fire" into orbit, take note: NASA's call for astronauts typically means thousands respond to such an invite. A small percentage makes the first cut. From there, further screening leads to a handful of selectees, whittled down by an Astronaut Selection Board.

For example, following an extensive year-and-a-half outreach, NASA announced a new group of potential astronauts in 2013. Eight candidates were selected to be NASA's newest astronaut trainees, picked from the second largest number of applications NASA had ever received—more than 6,100 people.

That group of eight is undergoing a wide array of technical training at space centers around the globe to prepare for missions to low Earth orbit, as well as deep space missions, such as to an asteroid and Mars.

BEING ALL YOU CAN BE

If persistence is what makes you tick—enough to set your sights on an astronaut career—here are the basics. It is worth noting that the majority of astronauts who made the grade had Boy Scout or Girl Scout training in their past. Quite clearly, individuals who were involved in such programs also acquired character-building traits—some of the same qualities NASA is on the lookout for in its astronaut crews.

College preparatory classes in high school are a step in the right direction. Heavy emphasis on math and science-related courses is a must. Striving for the highest grades possible is an obvious condition. Having a clear direction by the third or fourth year in high school of what specific field you find of greatest interest is critical. Thanks to the variance of fields from which NASA needs astronauts, people skillful in such areas as physical science, engineering, biology, and chemistry are also in demand.

While NASA demands a minimum requirement of a bachelor's degree for its astronauts, a majority of those selected have continued their education to the post-graduate level. Beyond a degree, at least three years of professional work experience in a chosen field is mandatory. An advanced degree is desirable and may be substituted for all or part of the experience requirement (i.e., master's degree = one year of work experience, doctoral degree = three years of experience).

KNOCKING ON NASA's DOOR

NASA selected the first group of U.S. space travelers—the Mercury astronauts—in 1959. From 500 candidates, with the required jet aircraft flight experience and engineering training and a height of less than 5 feet 11 inches, seven military men constituted the nation's premier astronaut corps. What does height have to do with ascending to the heavens? As the first American to orbit Earth, astronaut John Glenn, once said: "You didn't fly in the Mercury capsule, you wore it." Space travel has come a long way from single-person, two- and three-seat capsules, then the winged Space Shuttle, to today's multi-person Orion spacecraft.

By 1964, in fact, astronaut requirements had changed, and emphasis was placed on academic qualifications. In 1965, for instance, six scientist astronauts were selected from a group of 400 who had doctorates or equivalent experience in the natural sciences, medicine, or engineering.

The astronaut group named in 1978 was the first of the Space Shuttle flight crews and was composed of 15 pilots and 20 mission specialists. Six of these were women and four were members of minorities. Since that period of time, additional groups were selected that included a mix of pilots and missions specialists.

Hand-picked astronauts have slid into their seats as part of several human spaceflight projects: The Mercury, Gemini, Apollo, the Apollo-Soyuz Test Project (the first joint mission with the then Soviet Union), Skylab, the Space Shuttle effort, and today's Orion program.

And given the introduction of the NASA Orion spacecraft, the space agency is literally spreading its wings to fulfill new space exploration assignments that require human involvement.

The astronauts of the 21st century will continue to work aboard the *International Space Station* in cooperation with international partners; help to build and fly the new Orion Multi-Purpose Crew Vehicle (MPCV) designed for human deep space exploration; and further NASA's efforts to partner with industry to provide a commercial capability for space transportation to the space station.

The Orion vehicle draws from more than 50 years of past NASA human spaceflight experience and is being built and tested to meet the on-going needs of America's future human space exploration program. But keep in mind that Orion is not "Apollo déjà vu" in many regards.

Orion features dozens of technology advancements and innovations that have been incorporated into the spacecraft's subsystem and component design. Orion's life support, propulsion, thermal protection, and avionics systems, in combination with other deep space elements, will enable extended duration deep space missions.

On December 5, 2014, an uncrewed Orion spacecraft was lofted atop a Delta IV Heavy rocket from the Cape Canaveral Air Force Station's Space Launch Complex on a successful two-orbit, four-hour flight that tested many of the systems most critical to safety. More test flights of Orion, both unmanned and piloted, are on the manifest.

* * *

Here are some general guidelines to consider, according to the latest NASA information:

Want to be onboard a future NASA human spaceflight mission? If so, what is the best degree field to choose?

Among the academic fields considered qualifying for astronaut candidate positions, NASA does not recommend one over another or specify which might be more appropriate in the future. You should choose a field of study that is of interest to you; this will ensure that, whatever course your career takes, you will be prepared to do something that is personally satisfying.

Are there age restrictions?

There are no age restrictions for the program. Astronaut candidates selected in the past have ranged between the ages of 26 and 46, with the average age of 34.

Do you have to be a U.S. citizen to apply for the Astronaut Candidate Program?

Yes, you must be a U.S. citizen to apply for the program through NASA. Applicants with valid U.S. dual-citizenship are also eligible. It is not recommended that you change your citizenship solely for the purpose of being eligible for the Astronaut Candidate Program.

NASA does have international astronauts from the countries with which the U.S. space agency does have an international agreement; Canada, Japan, Russia, Brazil, and Europe select the international astronaut. Each of these countries has their own space agency.

What is the best college or university to attend?

NASA does not recommend one college or university over another, or specify which schools might best prepare an individual for the Astronaut Candidate Program. However, please remember that the college or university you attend must be an accredited institution.

Is flying experience necessary?

Flying experience is not a requirement. The Astronaut Candidate Program requires either three years of professional related experience, or 1,000 hours of pilot-in-command time in jet aircraft to meet the minimum qualification requirement. Jet aircraft experience is usually obtained through the military. Any type of flying experience-military or private is beneficial to have.

Are waivers granted for any of the medical requirements?

No, NASA does not grant waivers for the medical requirements. When qualifying astronauts for spaceflight, NASA must look at not only what is required for normal spaceflight operations, but also what each astronaut would require should serious, even life threatening, problems develop. For maximum crew safety, each crewmember must be free of medical conditions that would either impair the person's ability to participate in, or be aggravated by, spaceflight, as determined by NASA physicians.

Is it better to apply as a civilian or through the military?

Military experience is not a requirement for the Astronaut Candidate Program. Active duty military personnel must submit applications for the Astronaut Candidate Program through their respective service. After preliminary screening by the military, a small number of applications are submitted to NASA for further consideration. If selected, military personnel are detailed to NASA for a selected period of time.

What is the annual salary for astronauts?

Salaries for civilian astronaut candidates are based on the federal government's general schedule pay scale for grades GS-11 through GS-14. The grade is determined in accordance with each individual's academic achievements and experience. Currently a GS-11 starts at $64,724 per year and a GS-14 can earn up to $141,715 per year.

For more specific details on NASA's astronaut selection program, go to: http://astronauts.nasa.gov/.

APPENDIX A: LEARNING THE LANGUAGE
KEY SPACE TERMS AND ACRONYMS

• **Antenna**—A device for transmitting and receiving radio waves. Depending on its use and operating frequency, antennas can be a single piece of wire, a grid of wires, a sophisticated parabolic-shaped dish or an array of electronic elements.

• **Apogee**—The point at which a spacecraft is at its farthest point from the Earth's surface.

• **Astrobiology**—Study of life on planets.

• **Astronautics**—The science of space travel, including the building and operating of space vehicles.

• **Attitude**—The position of a spacecraft as determined by the inclination of its axis to some point of reference.

• **Attitude control**—The orientation of the satellite in relationship to the Earth and Sun.

• **Bandwidth**—A measure of spectrum frequency use or capacity.

• **Bioastronautics**—Study of the effects of space travel on plant or animal life.

• **Bus**—The electronic brain of a satellite.

• **C-band**—Frequency range from 4-8 GHz. Primarily used for satellite communications, for full-time satellite TV networks or raw satellite feeds

• **Celestial mechanics**—Study of orbital paths of celestial bodies under the influence of gravitational fields.

• **COTS**—Commercial off-the-shelf.

• **Cryogenic**—Generally refers to liquids or the use of liquids at super-cold temperatures.

• **DBS**—Direct broadcast satellite, such as direct-to-home television or radio.

• **Delta V**—Velocity changes that enable a space vehicle to change its trajectory.

• **DoD**—US Department of Defense.

• **Downlink data**—The frequency range utilized by the satellite to retransmit signals to Earth for reception.

• **DTH**—Acronym for direct-to-home. Refers to direct broadcast satellite television and radio services.

• **Earth station**—Term used to describe the combination of an antenna, low-noise amplifier, down-converter, and receiver electronics used to receive a signal transmitted by a satellite.

• **Eccentric orbit**—An elliptical orbit, one with a very high apogee and a low perigee.

• **Eclipse**—When a satellite passes through the line between Earth and the Sun or Earth and the Moon.

• **Equatorial orbit**—An orbit with a

plane parallel to the Earth's equator.

• **Escape velocity**—The velocity a vehicle must attain in order to overcome the gravitational field.

• **ESA**—European Space Agency.

• **Expendable launch vehicle (ELV)**—A rocket that can only be launched once and whose components cannot be refurbished for future use.

• **Fairing**—The area of the launch vehicle where a payload is attached until its release into orbit.

• **FCC**—Federal Communications Commission.

• **FEMA**—Federal Emergency Management Agency.

• **Footprint**—A map of the signal strength showing the power contours of equal signal strengths as they cover the Earth's surface.

• **Frequency**—Number of times that an alternating current goes through its complete cycle in one second of time.

• **Frequency coordination**—A process to eliminate frequency interference among different satellite systems or among terrestrial microwave systems and satellites.

• **FSS**—Fixed–satellite service— refers to services using satellites in geostationary orbit.

• **Fuel cell**—Miniature electric power plants.

• **GEO**—Geostationary Earth orbit or geosynchronous Earth orbit.

• **Geostationary Earth orbit**—The point in space at which an object will revolve at the same speed as a point on Earth. From Earth, the object appears to be stationary.

• **Geosynchronous Earth orbit**—See above.

• **GIS**—Geographical information system.

• **GPS**—Global Positioning System for satellites.

• **Guidance, navigation, and control (GN&C)**—System that measures the velocity and directory of the spacecraft, compares it with its memory, and issues commands for corrections.

• **Hypersonic**—Speeds faster than Mach 5 (five times the speed of sound).

• **Inclination**—The angle of an orbit. Equatorial orbit has an inclination of zero, a polar Earth orbit has an inclination of 90 degrees.

• **Insurance**—Multiple types of coverage exist to reduce financial risks related to the satellite, launch, and on-orbit operation.

• **Integration**—Technical activity regarding the combining of different systems and/or components, such as placing a satellite inside the launch vehicle.

• **Ka-band**—Frequency range from 26–40 GHz. Used for satellite communications

- **Ku-band**—Frequency range from 12–18 GHz. Used for satellite communications

- **L-band**—Frequency range from 1–2 GHz. Used for GPS carriers and also satellite mobile phones, such as Iridium; Inmarsat, etc.

- **Launch vehicle**—A vehicle that is used to deliver payloads from Earth to space. Also see entries for expendable launch vehicle and reusable launch vehicle.

- **LEO**—Low Earth orbit.

- **Man-rated/Human-rated**—Equipment considered reliable enough to be used by people.

- **Mobile satellite services (MSS)**—Satellite-based mobile telecommunications systems that provide coverage over extended areas including remote locations. These usually operate in a low- or near-Earth orbit to reduce signal delay.

- **Mux/Demux**—A multiplexer combines several different signals (e.g., video, audio, data) onto a single communications channel for transmission. Demultiplexing separates each signal at the receiving end.

- **NOAA**—National Oceanic and Atmospheric Administration.

- **Orbit**—The path of a body under the influence of gravitational or other force around another body.

- **Orbital period**—The time it takes to complete one orbit.

- **Orbital velocity**—The speed required to establish and maintain a spacecraft in orbit.

- **Payload**—The cargo that is being carried for a mission.

- **Perigee**—The point in an orbit at which the spacecraft is closest to Earth.

- **Period**—The amount of time that it takes a satellite to complete one revolution of its orbit.

- **Polar orbit**—An orbit with its plane aligned parallel with the polar axis of Earth.

- **R&D**—Research and development.

- **RDT&E**—Research, development, test, and evaluation.

- **Receiver**—An electronic device that enables a particular satellite signal to be separated from all others being received by an Earth station, and converts the signal into a format for video, voice, or data.

- **Remote sensing**—The collection of data from a distant location. Remotely sensed data is typically collected from sensors located on an aircraft, balloon, or spacecraft.

- **Reusable launch vehicle (RLV)**—A rocket that, after placing its payload in space, is returned to Earth and refurbished for future flights.

- **RF**—Radiofrequency.

- **Rocket**—See launch vehicle.

• **Satellite**—Sophisticated electronic device operating outside Earth that enables a variety of activities.

• **Sensor**—An electronic device that monitors or collects data.

• **Slot**—The longitudinal position in geostationary orbit at which a communications satellite is located.

• **Sounding rocket**—A research rocket that sends equipment to the upper atmosphere, takes measurements, and returns to Earth.

• **Specific impulse**—A means of expressing rocket performance.

• **Spectrum**—Range of electromagnetic radio frequencies used in the transmission of voice, data, and video.

• **Spin-off**—Commercial or other benefits derived from space research.

• **Support services**—Includes technical and business support activities, such as legal and licensing, finance, consulting, and publishing.

• **Telemetry**—Technique whereby information on the health, activity, and location of a spacecraft is measured and transmitted to Earth.

• **Teleport**—A facility that provides uplink and downlink services.

• **Three-axis stabilization**—Type of spacecraft stabilization in which the body maintains a fixed attitude relative to the orbital track and Earth's surface.

• **Transfer orbit**—A highly elliptical orbit that is used as an intermediate stage for placing satellites in geostationary orbit.

• **Transponder**—A combination receiver, frequency converter, and transmitter package that is a physical part of a communications satellite.

• **Turnkey**—A system that is supplied, installed, and sometimes managed by one vendor or manufacturer.

• **Uplink data**—Earth to space communications pathway.

• **USAF**—United States Air Force.

• **Value-added provider**—An organization that modifies an existing product or data source before delivering it to the end customer. In remote sensing, value-added providers manipulate the raw data into more usable forms, such as a graphical map.

• **VSAT**—Acronym for very small aperture terminal. Refers to small Earth stations. Many are used to connect remote locations with a central computer, such as those for ATM bank machines, credit card processing, etc. Can also refer to systems enabling consumer / remote access to broadband.

• **Window**—Limited time period during which a space vehicle can be launched, if it is to accomplish its mission.

APPENDIX B:
COMMERCIAL ORGANIZATIONS INVOLVED WITH SPACE

In this appendix
Some of the 2,000 organizations in the space industry are listed.

Advantech Wireless
Main:	http://www.advantechwireless.com
HQ:	657 Orly Ave, Montreal QC H9P 1G1 Canada
	Tel: +1 (514) 420-0045

Manufactures electronics for broadband connectivity, broadcast solutions, and backhaul using satellite (HPAs, SSPA, BUCs, DVB-RCS VSAT hubs and terminals, antennas, converters, and satellite modems.

Aerojet Rocketdyne
Main:	http://www.rocket.com
Career:	http://www.rocket.com/careers
HQ:	2001 Aerojet Road Rancho, Cordova, CA 95742-6418
	Tel: +1 (703) 650-0270

Provides propulsion and energetics to the space, missile defense, strategic, tactical missile and armaments, including the engines that were used on Apollo and the Space Shuttle as well as for future space efforts.

Locations: Sacramento, CA; Carlstadt, NJ; Camden, AR; Canoga Park, CA; Gainesville, VA; Hill AFB, UT; Washington, DC; West Palm Beach, FL; Stennis Space Center, MS; Socorro, NM; Redmond, WA; Culpepper, VA; Jonesborough, TN; Huntsville AL.

Aerospace Corporation
Main:	http://www.aerospace.org
Career:	http://www.aerospace.org/careers/
HQ:	2310 E. El Segundo Blvd., El Segundo, CA 90245-4691
	Tel: +1 (310) 336-5000

Operates a federally funded research-and-development center for the U.S. Air Force and the National Reconnaissance Office and supports all national security space programs. Also performs projects for civil agencies, such as NASA and NOAA, commercial companies, universities, and international organizations in the national interest.

Locations: Albuquerque, NM; Aurora, CO; Cape Canaveral, FL; Chantilly, VA; Colorado Springs, CO; Houston, TX, Huntsville, AL; Pasadena, CA; Peterson AFB, CO; Vandenberg AFB, CA; Wright-Patterson AFB, OH.

Ai Solutions

Main: http://www.ai-solutions.com
Career: http://www.ai-solutions.com/Careers/
HQ: 10001 Derekwood Ln., Suite 215, Lanham, MD 20706
            Tel: +1 (301) 306-1756

Engineering, science and IT professionals nationwide serving civilian, defense, and commercial customers in the areas of flight dynamics, space operations, ground system software, information technology, and systems engineering for launch vehicles, missiles and satellites.

Regional offices: Cape Canaveral, FL; Huntsville, AL, and Colorado Springs, CO.

Analytical Graphics

Main: http://www.agi.com
Career: http://www.agi.com/careers/
HQ: 220 Valley Creek Blvd., Exton, PA 19341
            Tel: +1 (610) 981-8000

Major locations: Washington, DC-area; Colorado Springs, CO; southern California.

Software to model, analyze, and visualize space, defense, and intelligence systems.

Andrews Space

Main: http://andrews-space.com/
Career: http://andrews-space.com/careers
HQ: 3415 S. 116th St., Suite 123, Tukwila, WA 98168
            Tel: +1 (206) 342-9934

Andrews' technical competencies include product/system development, space system design, rapid prototyping, propulsion system design, systems engineering, and business analysis.

Apollo Microwaves Ltd

Main: http://www.apollomw.com
HQ: 1650 Trans-Canada Hwy, Dorval, QC H9P 1H7 Canada
                Tel: +1 (514) 421-2211

Passive microwave components and subsystems from 900 MHz to 60GHz.

Applied Physics Laboratory at Johns Hopkins University

Main: http://www.jhuapl.edu/
Career: http://www.jhuapl.edu/employment/default.asp
HQ: 11100 Johns Hopkins Road, Laurel, MD 20723
                Tel: +1 (240) 228-5000

APL focuses primarily on space physics and planetary sciences and its 5,000+ scientists and engineers and analysts have, for more than 70 years, served as trusted advisors and technical experts to government, ensuring the reliability of complex technologies that safeguard the nation's security and advance the frontiers of space. APL conducts research and space exploration and develops and applies space science, engineering, and technology, including the production of one-of-a-kind spacecraft, instruments, and subsystems. APL has designed, developed, and launched 64 spacecraft and more than 150 space instruments.

Artel LLC

Main: http://www.artelllc.com
HQ: 13665 Dulles Technology Dr, Herndon, VA 20171
                Tel: +1 (703) 620-1700

Provides a full portfolio of satellite and terrestrial network communications and infrastructure, cybersecurity, risk management and IT solutions.

ASC Signal Corporation

Main: http://www.ascsignal.com
HQ: 1120 Jupiter Rd, Suite 102, Plano TX 75074
                Tel: +1 (214) 291-7654

Supplier of satellite earth station equipment from 3.5 meters to 9.4 meters and operating in the C-, K-, Ka-, Ku-, and X-bands.

Astrotech Corporation

Main: http://astrotechcorp.com/
HQ: 401 Congress Ave, Suite 1650, Austin, Texas 78701
Tel: +1 (512) 485-9530

Astrotech, formerly SPACEHAB, Inc., has for more than 25 years prepared and sent satellites, cargo, and science into space.

AvL Technologies

Main: http://www.avltech.com
HQ: 15 North Merrimon Ave, Asheville, NC 28804
Tel: +1 (828) 250-9950

Mobile satellite antennas and positioners for communications products.

AVCOM of Virginia, Inc

Main: http://www.avcomofva.com
HQ: 7729 Pocoshock Way, Richmond VA 23235
Tel: +1 (804) 794-2500

Test equipment for the satellite communications industry

Ball Aerospace

Main: http://www.ballaerospace.com/
Career: http://www.ballaerospace.com/page.jsp?page=7
HQ: 10 Longs Peak Drive, Broomfield, CO 80021
Tel: +1 (303) 939-6100

Ball Aerospace designs, develops, and manufactures spacecraft, instruments and sensors, RF and microwave technologies, data exploitation solutions and a variety of advanced aerospace technologies and products.

Major locations: Boulder, CO; Washington, DC; Chantilly, VA; Albuquerque, NM.

Barrios Technology

Main: http://www.barrios.com/pages/home.asp
Career: http://www.barrios.com/careers.asp
HQ: 16441 Space Center Blvd., Suite B-100, Houston, TX 77058
Tel: +1 (281) 280-1900

Barrios provides a full spectrum of engineering, operations and related technology services in support of the aerospace community with strengths in engineering, program planning and control, and software engineering.

Bigelow Aerospace

Main: http://www.bigelowaerospace.com/
Career: http://www.bigelowaerospace.com/careers
HQ: 1899 W. Brooks Ave, North Las Vegas, NV 89032
                   Tel: +1 (702) 639-4440

The firm is developing patented expandable habitats. The Bigelow Aerospace Mission Control Center monitors and operates the company's spacecraft currently in orbit and will control Bigelow Aerospace's future space facilities. Data and imagery are transmitted into Mission Control from the two Bigelow Aerospace spacecraft currently orbiting the Earth—*Genesis I* and *Genesis II*.

Blue Origin LLC

Main: http://www.blueorigin.com
Career: http://www.blueorigin.com/careers/
HQ: 21218 76th Ave S, Kent, WA 98032
                   Tel: +1 (253) 437-9300

Blue Origin, LLC, founded by Amazon.com CEO Jeff Bezos, is developing technologies to enable human access to space at dramatically lower cost and increased reliability. This is a long-term effort, and the company is pursuing it incrementally, step by step; currently focused on developing reusable launch vehicles utilizing rocket-powered Vertical Take-off and Vertical Landing (VTVL) technology.

Boeing

Main: http://www.boeing.com
Space Group: http://www.boeing.com/boeing/space

Careers: http://www.boeing.com/boeing/careers/index.page?
                   http://jobs-boeing.com/
Corporate: 100 North Riverside, Chicago, IL 60606
                   Tel: +1 (312) 544-2000

Boeing employs more than 50,000 people worldwide in the areas of human spaceflight, space transportation, military space and security, satellite systems and services, and heavy lift launch vehicles. The Space & Intelligence Systems Group is involved with commercial satellites, commercial satellite services; GPS satellites, Tracking and Data Relay Satellites, Wideband Global Satcom satellites, and the X-37B Orbital Test vehicle. The Space Exploration Group is involved with space launch services, launch products and services, the Boeing Space Crew Transportation system; and the *International Space Station.*

Major locations: Huntsville, AL; Seal Beach, CA; Huntington Beach, CA; El Segundo, CA: Long Beach, CA; Kennedy Space Center, FL; Houston, TX; Washington, DC; Annapolis Junction, MD.

Booz Allen & Hamilton

Main: http://www.boozallen.com
Careers: http://www.boozallen.com/careers
HQ: 8283 Greensboro Drive, McLean, VA 22102
                 Tel: +1 (703) 902-5000

Strategy and technology consulting to help defense, civil, and intelligence agencies address the technical, cost, schedule, and risk aspects of space systems development.

Braxton Technologies

Main: http://www.braxtontech.com
HQ: 6 North Tejon Street, Suite 220, Colorado Springs, CO 80903
                 Tel: +1 (719) 380-8488

Hardware and software components necessary for complete ground system implementation, from front-end communications processors and crypto controllers to user workstations for satellite ground systems, space, atmospheric, and ground C2 missions. .

C-Com Satellite Systems

Main: http://www.c-comsat.com
HQ: 2574 Sheffield Rd, Ottawa ON K1B 3V7, Canada
                 Tel: +1 (613) 745-4110

With over 6000 systems deployed worldwide, the firm develops and deploys mobile satellite-based technology for the delivery of two-way high-speed Internet, VoIP and video services into vehicles.

ComDev

Main: http://www.comdev.ca or www.comdevinternational.com

Careers: http://www.comdev.ca/careers
Canada HQ: 155 Sheldon Drive Cambridge, ON N1R 7H6, CANADA
                  Tel: +1 (519) 622-2300
US HQ: 2333 Utah Ave., El Segundo, CA 90245
                  Tel: +1 (424) 456-8000

A global designer and manufacturer of space hardware including scientific instrumentation and payloads, optical surveillance payloads, spacecraft bus for microsatellite solutions as well as being world leaders in the production of space-qualified passive microwave equipment, specialized electronics and optical subsystems. More than 1,200 employees at facilities in Canada, the United Kingdom and the United States.

Communications and Power Industries (CPI)

Main: http://www.cpii.com
HQ: 811 Hansen Way, Palo Alto CA 94304
                  Tel: +1 (650) 846-2900

CPI manufactures TWTAs, KPAs, SSPAs, high power BUCs, and LNAs for various satellite applications.

Comtech EF Data

Main: http://www.comtechefdata.com
HQ: 2114 W 7th St, Tempe AZ 85281
                  Tel: +1 (480) 333-2200

Products for satellite bandwidth efficiency and link optimization.

Comtech Telecommunications Corp

Main: http://www.comtechtel.com
HQ: 68 South Service Rd, Suite 230, Melville NY 11747

Manufactures satellite electronics including modems, solid sate amplifiers, traveling wave tube amplifiers, and over-the-horizon microwave systems.

Comtech Xicom Technology, Inc.

Main: http://www.xicomtech.com
HQ: 3550 Bassett St, Santa Clara, CA 95054
                  Tel: +1 (408) 213-3000

Product line of KPAs, TWTAs, SSPAs, and BUCs for satellite uplink.

CSC North American Public Sector

Main: http://www.csc.com
Careers: http://www.csc.com/contact_us/ds/88858-
               contact_information_for_careers
HQ: 3170 Fairview Park Drive, Falls Church, VA 22042
               Tel: +1 (703) 876-1000

CSC provides information technology (IT) services and solutions with major contracts at NASA and the Air Force.

DigitalGlobe

Main: http://www.digitalglobe.com/
Careers: http://www.digitalglobe.com/careers
HQ: 1601 Dry Creek Drive, Suite 260, Longmont, CO 80503
               Tel: +1 (303) 684.4000

DigitalGlobe is a global provider of commercial high-resolution Earth imagery products and geospatial solution services. Sourced from its advanced satellite constellation, its imagery solutions support a wide variety of uses within defense and intelligence, civil agencies, mapping and analysis, environmental monitoring, oil and gas exploration, infrastructure management, Internet portals and navigation technology.

DirecTV

Main: http://www.directv.com
Careers: http://www.directv.com/DTVAPP/content/careers
HQ: 2230 E. Imperial Hwy, El Segundo, CA 90245
               Tel: +1 (855) 802-3473

DIRECTV is one of the world's leading providers of digital television entertainment services. Many of the more than 16,000 employees operate the broadcast centers on the ground, monitor satellites in space, or provide customer service.

Corporate offices in El Segundo, CA; New York City; and Denver, CO.
Broadcast centers in Castle Rock, CO; Long Beach, CA; and Marina del Rey, CA.
Customer contact and sales offices in ID, CO, WV, AL, MT, OK, GA, IL.

Draper Laboratory

Main: http://www.draper.com
Careers: http://www.draper.com/our_culture.html
HQ: 555 Technology Square, Cambridge, MA 02139-3563
                  Tel: +1 (617) 258-1000

Draper is a not-for-profit research-and-development laboratory focused on the design, development, and deployment of advanced technological solutions for the nation's most challenging and important problems in security, space exploration, healthcare, and energy. Expertise includes guidance, navigation, and control systems; fault-tolerant computing; advanced algorithms and software solutions; modeling and simulation; and MEMS and multichip module technology.

Other locations: Cambridge, MA; Houston, TX; Washington, DC; Huntsville, AL.

EchoStar Corporation

Main: http://www.echostar.com
Career: http://www.echostarcareers.com/
HQ: 100 Inverness Terrace East, Englewood, CO 80112
                  Tel: +1 (303) 706-4000

EchoStar Satellite Services provides advanced satellite communications solutions from video distribution, data communications, and backhaul services to the delivery of television channels for direct-to-homes satellite providers and broadcasters. EchoStar's wholly owned subsidiary, Hughes, is the world's leading provider of satellite broadband services, delivering network technologies and managed services in more than 100 countries.

Echostar Satellite Services

Main: http://www.echostarsatelliteservices.com
HQ: 100 Inverness Terrace East, Englewood, CO 80112
                  Tel: +1 (866) 359-8804

Provides communications solutions including video distribution, data communications, and backhaul services.

Emerging Markets Communications
Main: http://www.emc-corp.net
HQ: 777 Briskell Ave, Suite 1150, Miami, FL 33130
                 Tel: +1 (305) 539-1358

EMC operates in 140 countries with 300+ employees that deliver satellite and terrestrial networks and services to telecom carriers, banks, energy, government, NGOs, and enterprises.

Eutelsat
Main: http://www.eutelsatamerica.com
US HQ: 1776 I Street, NW; Suite 810, Washington DC 20006
                 Tel: +1 (202) 559-4330

With a fleet of 34 satellites, Eutelsat is Europe's leading satellite operator and the third largest globally.

Exelis (Acquisition by Harris Proposed in February 2015)
Main: http://www.exelisinc.com/
Career: http://www.exelisinc.com/careers/
HQ: 1650 Tysons Blvd. Suite 1700, McLean, VA 22102
                 Tel +1 (703) 790-6300

Geospatial: 400 Initiative Drive, P.O. Box 60488, Rochester, NY 14606
                 Tel: +1 (585) 269-5600
Weather and Space Sciences: 1919 W. Cook Road, Fort Wayne, IN 46801
                 Tel: +1 (260) 451-6000
GPS Navigation: 77 River Road, Clifton, NJ 07014
                 Tel: +1 (973) 284-3000
Visual Information Solutions: 4990 Pearl East Circle, Boulder, CO 80301
                 Tel: +1 (303) 786-9900
Geospatial Information Solutions-Enterprise Products:
                 7007 Harbour View Blvd., Suite 101, Suffolk, VA 23435
                 Tel: +1 (757) 483-0226

Exelis employees nearly 10,000 people and is a diversified, top-tier global aerospace, defense and information solutions company leader in positioning and navigation, sensors, air traffic management solutions, image processing and distribution, communications and information systems; and focused on strategic growth in the areas of critical networks, ISR and analytics, electronic warfare and composite aerostructures.

Exelis Geospatial Systems provides intelligence, Earth and space science, and commercial aerospace arenas with a wide ranges of capabilities in the image capture, remote sensing and navigation industry.

Error! Hyperlink reference not valid.GPS Payload, Receiver and Control Systems: Our Positioning, Navigation and Timing (PNT) business is a total GPS navigation systems supplier providing GPS
payload, receiver and control solutions. We have developed more than 50 GPS satellite payloads that have been on every GPS satellite ever accumulated nearly 700 years of on-orbit life without a single mission-related failure due to our equipment.

Space-based Intelligence, Surveillance and Reconnaissance: Precision optics and structures with specialized capabilities including high reliability remote sensing payloads for ground, air and space, offering active and motion imaging, anti-jam signal generation data encryption, information processing and system performance modeling and simulation. We also provide solutions that map and monitor the earth for a variety of commercial and governmental users.

Garmin International

Main: http://www.garmin.com
Career: http://www.garmin.com/en-US/company/careers/
HQ: 1200 E. 151st St. Olathe, KS 66062-3426
                 Tel: +1 (913) 397-8200

With more than 9200 employees in 32 countries, Garmin has pioneered new GPS navigation and wireless devices and applications that are designed for people who live an active lifestyle. Garmin serves five primary business units, including automotive, aviation, fitness, marine, and outdoor recreation.

General Dynamics AIS

Main: http://www.gd-ais.com
                 http://www.gd-ais.com/Products/Space-Electronics
Careers: http://www.gd-ais.com/Careers

AIS HQ: 12450 Fair Lakes Circle, Fairfax, VA
                 Tel: +1 (703) 263-2800
                 8201 East McDowell Road, Scottsdale, AZ 85257
                 1450 Academy Park Loop, Colorado Springs, CO 80910
                 Tel: +1 (719) 313-5900

2721 Technology Dr, Suite 400, Annapolis Junction, MD 20701
Tel: +1 (240) 456-5500
911 Elkridge Landing Road, Linthicum, MD 21090
14700 Lee Road Chantilly, VA 20151

General Dynamics has more than 50 years of experience designing and manufacturing high reliability space electronics for NASA and the Department of Defense; manufactures flight-proven subsystem and components including space communications and data handling electronics, miniaturized power components and on-board software development. It supplies the tracking, telemetry and control (TT&C), precision navigation and timing, and crosslink equipment for missions of human spaceflight, near-Earth observation, lunar and deep space exploration.

General Dynamics C4 Systems

Main: http://www.gdc4s.com
               http://www.gdc4s.com/services/satellite-communication-services.html
Careers: http://www.gdc4s.com/careers.html
HQ: 8201 E. McDowell Road, Scottsdale, AZ 85257
               Tel: +1 (877) 449-0600
SpacePlex   4600 Research Park Circle, Las Cruces, NM 88001
               Tel: +1 (575) 541-7700
               430 National Business Parkway, Annapolis Junction, MD 20701
               Tel: +1 (443) 755-8000
               6000 Technology Drive, Bldg. 6, Huntsville, AL 35805
               Tel: +1 (256) 890-2147
               2900 Crystal Drive, Suite 510, Arlington, VA 22202
               Tel: +1 (703) 769-1500

Complex command, control, computing and communications challenges for U. S. government customers General Dynamics Satellite Communication Services provides access to the world via mobile and fixed commercial communications products and services.

Gigasat

Main: http://www.ultra-gigasat.com/
HQ: 2 Beach Rd, Annapolis MD 21405
               Tel: +1 (443) 994-2100

Manufactures fixed, mobile, and flyaway satellite earth station antennas from 0.5m to 4.5m.

Globalstar

Main: http://www.globalstar.com/en/
Careers: http://www.globalstar.com/en/index.php?cid=8700
HQ: 300 Holiday Square Blvd., Covington, Louisiana 70433
                Tel: +1 (985) 335-1538

Globalstar operates a network of satellites to provide mobile satellite voice and data services to government, commercial and recreational users in more than 120 countries around the world.

Globecomm Systems

Main: http://www.globecommsystems.com/
Career: http://www.globecommsystems.com/about/career.shtml
HQ: 45 Oser Avenue, Hauppauge, NY 11788-3816
                Tel: +1 (866) 499-0223

Globecomm designs, integrates, and offers end-to-end communications solutions using fixed and portable Earth stations as well as providing teleport and network services.

Globecomm Maritime   210 Malapardis Rd, Suite 202, Cedar Knolls, NJ 07927
                        Tel: +1 (973) 889-8990
Globecomm Government   9115 Whiskey Bottom Rd, Suite H, Laurel, MD 20723
                        Tel: +1 (866) 498-5650
Comsource   8430 Gas House Pike, Frederick, MD 21701
                        Tel: +1 (240) 379-1700

GMV

Main: http://www.gmv.com
US HQ: 2400 Research Blvd, Ste 390, Rockville, MD, 20850
                Tel. +1 (240) 252-2320

Provides engineering, software development, and systems integration in the areas of satellite control, flight dynamics, mission data processing, mission analysis, mission planning, and navigation systems and applications

Harris Corporation

Main: http://www.harris.com
Career: http://www.harris.com/careers/
HQ: 1025 W NASA Boulevard, Melbourne, FL 32919
               Tel: +1 (321) 727-9100

Government Communications Systems
               2400 Palm Bay Road, NE Palm Bay, FL 32905
               Tel: +1 (321) 727-9100

Harris is an international communications and information technology company serving government and commercial markets with $5 billion in annual revenue and about 14,000 employees—including 6,000 engineers and scientists. Harris is involved with the architecture, design and development of highly specialized satellite antennas, structures, phased arrays, and onboard processors that enable next-generation satellite systems for military, intelligence, government, and commercial customers.

Harris CapRock Communications

Main: http://www.harriscaprock.com
Careers   http://www.harriscaprock.com/careers.php
HQ: 4400 S. Sam Houston Pkwy East, Houston, TX 77048
               Tel: +1 (832) 668-2300
Harris CapRock Govt   2235 Monroe Street, Herndon, VA 20171
               Tel: +1 (703) 673-1400
Harris CapRock Maritime 1025 West NASA Blvd., Melbourne, FL 32919
               Tel: +1 (321) 674-4750

Harris CapRock Communications is a global provider of managed satellite and terrestrial communications solutions specifically for remote and harsh environments including the energy, government and maritime markets. The firm owns and operates a robust global infrastructure that includes teleports on six continents, five 24/7 customer support centers, local presence in 23 countries and more than 275 global field service personnel supporting customer locations across North America, Central and South America, Europe, West Africa and Asia Pacific.

Honeywell Aerospace

Main:	http://www. Honeywell.com
Space:	http://aerospace.honeywell.com/markets/space
Careers:	http://www.careersathoneywell.com/en/aerospace
Aerospace HQ:	21111 N. 19th Ave, Phoenix, AZ 85072
	Tel: +1 (602) 365-3099

Honeywell Aerospace is a $10 billion division of Honeywell that manufactures aircraft engines and avionics, as well as a producer of auxiliary power units and other aviation products.

Operations in Maryland and around the country.

Honeywell Space Engineering and Operations
HTSI, the nation's most experienced space systems operations company has more than 50 years' experience in the mission engineering, designing, fabricating, installing, operating, and maintaining satellite command and control systems; integration and testing of spaceflight hardware and software; antenna RF solutions, mission engineering, and satellite network operations maintenance.

Honeywell Space Navigation and Microelectronics
More than 40 years experience producing guidance, navigation and control products ranging from complex launch vehicle inertial navigation to versatile off-the-shelf inertial measurement units. Honeywell's radiation hardened electronics products and technology provide aerospace system and electrical designers a strategically hardened family of products to increase performance. Honeywell environmental control and life support systems have logged more than 500 million aircraft flight hours since 1945 and 35,000 flight hours in space.

Hughes Network Systems, A Subsidiary of Echostar

Main:	http://www.hughes.com/
Career:	http://www.hughes.com/company/careers
HQ:	11717 Exploration Lane, Germantown, MD 20876
	Tel: +1 (301) 428-5500

Hughes provides satellite broadband for home and office. This includes the manufacture and design of satellite networking products and services including very small aperture terminals (VSAT), high-speed Internet service, and the design and development of mobile satellite systems and related terminals.

iDirect

Main: http://www.idirect.net
HQ: 13865 Sunrise Valley Dr, Herndon VA 20171
               Tel: +1 (703) 648-8000

IP-based satellite communications company providing technology, hardware, software, and services that enable VSAT service providers to optimize their networks.

ILC Dover

Main: http://www.ilcdover.com/space
Careers: http://www.ilcdover.com/careers
HQ: One Moonwalker Road, Frederica, DE 19946-2080
               Tel: +1 (302) 335-3911

ILC has supplied all the space suits for NASA since project Apollo. The customized impact bags helped safely land the first rover on Mars.

InSpace 21

Main: http://www.inspace21.com/
Career: http://www.inspace21.com/careers.html
HQ: 3170 Fairview Park Drive, Falls Church, VA 22042
               Tel: +1 (703) 876-1000

A CSC and Honeywell joint venture, it provides operations, engineering, sustainment and logistics solutions at ranges including Cape Canaveral, AUTEC, Wallops, Nellis, and White Sands.

Intelsat

Main: http://www.intelsat.com
Career: http://www.intelsat.com/careers/
HQ: 7900 Tysons One Place, McLean, VA 22102-5972
               Phone: +1 (703) 559-6800

Intelsat is the largest provider of satellite services worldwide and for 50 years it has delivered information and entertainment for many of the world's leading media and network companies, multinational corporations, Internet service providers and governmental agencies. Opportunities exist in aerospace, engineering, sales, finance, information technology and several other disciplines.

Locations: The firm has sales offices around the world.

Intelsat General

Main:	http://www.intelsatgeneral.com
HQ:	7900 Tysons One Place, Suite 12, McLean, VA 22102
Tel:	+1 (703) 270-4200

A wholly owned subsidy of Intelsat, the firm provides satellite communications solutions to military and government customers over Intelsat's fleet of satellites.

ILS

Main:	http://www.ilslaunch.com/
Careers:	http://www.ilslaunch.com/careers
HQ:	1875 Explorer Street, Suite 700, Reston, VA 20190
	Tel: +1 (571) 633-7400

International Launch Services provides mission management and launch services for the global commercial satellite industry using the premier heavy lift vehicle, the Proton, and other vehicles

Inmarsat

Main:	http://www.inmarsat.com
Careers:	http://www.inmarsat.com/about-us/careers/our-offices/
US Addresses	58 Inverness Drive East, Suite 100, Englewood, CO 80112
	Tel: +1 (303) 397-7500
	1101 Connecticut Avenue NW, Washington, DC 20006
	Tel: +1 (202) 248-5150

Headquartered in London UK, Inmarsat is a global satellite operator with offices and operational centers in more than 40 countries employing more than 1500 people. The firm offers a portfolio of global satcom solutions and value-added services to keep people connected on land, sea or in the air.

US offices in Washington, DC; Stafford TX, Seattle WA, Scott LA, Plantation FL, New Orleans LA, Miami FL, Houston TX, Herdon VA, Englewood CO,

Iridium Communications Inc.

Main:	http://www.iridium.com
HQ:	1750 Tysons Boulevard, Suite 1400, McLean, VA 22102
	Tel: +1 (703) 287-7400

Business Operations: 8440 South River Parkway, Tempe, AZ 85284
Tel: +1 (480) 752-1000

Iridium's low-Earth orbiting cross-linked satellites—the world's largest commercial constellation—operate as a fully meshed network that reaches over oceans, through airways and across the polar regions. Iridium solutions are suited for industries such as maritime, aviation, government/military, emergency/humanitarian services, mining, forestry, oil and gas, heavy equipment, transportation and utilities.

Kratos Defense & Security Services
Main: http://www.kratosdefense.com
Corporate: 5971 Kingstowne Village Pkwy, Ste 200, Alexandria VA 22315
               Tel: +1 (858) 812-7300

Provides earth station solutions for national security platforms and programs.

Kratos ISI
Main: http://www.kratosTTS.com/KISI
HQ: 5200 Philadelphia Way, Lanham MD 20706
               Tel: +1 (443) 539-5008

Provides turnkey earth stations, and products, systems, and services for satellite command and control, telemetry and digital signal processing, data communications, enterprise network management, and communications assurance.

Kratos Networks
Main: http://www.kratosnetworks.com
Corporate: 5971 Kingstowne Village Pkwy, Ste 200, Alexandria VA 22315
               Tel: +1 (858) 812-7300

Products organize and manage communications performance across hybrid networks.

KVH Industries
Main: http://www.kvh.com/
Careers: http://www.kvh.com/About-Us/Careers.aspx
HQ: 50 Enterprise Center, Middletown, RI 02842
               Tel: +1 (401) 847 3327
Guidance & Stabilization:
               8412 W. 185th Street, Tinley Park, IL 60487-9237
               Tel: +1 (708) 444 2800

KVH Industries is a manufacturer of solutions that provide global high-speed Internet, television, and voice services via satellite to mobile users at sea and on land. These solutions include the mini-VSAT broadband network, TracPhone satellite communications systems, and TracVision satellite television systems. KVH is also a premier manufacturer of high performance sensors and integrated inertial systems for defense and commercial guidance and stabilization applications.

L-3 Communications

Main: http://www.l-3com.com
Careers: http://www.l-3com.com/careers
HQ: 600 Third Avenue, New York, NY 10016
                Tel: +1 (212) 697-1111
Locations: http://www.l-3com.com/locations.html

L-3 is a prime contractor in aerospace systems and national security solutions and operates under dozens of independent operating companies that are involved with satellite communications and electronics. A list of all divisions can be found at http://www.l-3com.com/divisions-a-z

Locations: http://www.l-3com.com/locations.html. Divisions include Huntsville Operations (AL); Communications Systems West (Salt Lake City, UT); Telemetry-East (Bristol, PA); Cincinnati Electronics (Mason, OH); Narda Satellite Networks (Hauppague, NY); Narda Microwave East (Hauppauge, NY); Space & Navigation (Budd Lake, NJ); Communications Systems—East (Camden, NJ); ESSCO (Ayer, MA); Wolf Coach (Ayer, MA); Electrodynamcis (Rolling Meadows, IL); Coleman Aerospace (Orlando, FL); Datron Advanced Technologies (Simi Valley, CA); Telemetry-West (San Diego, CA).

Leidos

Main: https://www.leidos.com/space
Career: https://www.leidos.com/careers
HQ: 11951 Freedom Drive Reston, VA 20190
                Tel: +1 (571) 526-6000
Major locations throughout the United States

Conducts mission analyses to define requirements; provide design, development, integration and test; and on-orbit support to meet program needs. Leidos scientists, engineers and programmers provide a full range of engineering and integration management support for military and civil space customers. They also provide systems engineering and integration efforts for the U.S. Air Force GPS Directorate, MILSATCOM, and Space-Based Infrared Systems (SBIRS) programs. In addition, Leidos provides advanced space mission planning expertise to the U.S. military and to space research centers developing and operating robotic missions in near-earth orbit, those bound for other bodies in the solar system and for missions of human exploration of the Moon and Mars.

Space Sustainment and Operations teams provide support for U.S. Air Force space systems including SBIRS, GPS, and MILSATCOM in the areas of reliability, maintainability, and availability engineering, program environmental, safety, and health evaluation, operational safety, suitability, and effectiveness analyses. Operations support includes efforts to enhance military operations, providing field support, management, training, and developing product capabilities that enable productive incorporation of space-provided information and capabilities including space telemetry downlink operations and analysis, analytical expertise in decomposing data streams, and improving data quality and providing data analysis products.

Exploitation of Space Assets includes imagery and mapping management, and data dissemination to support military and civil operations. It constructs mapping and simulation products; supports NASA, NOAA, EPA, USGS, NGA, and other federal agencies, in a broad range of space, Earth, ocean, and atmospheric applied sciences and research.

Lockheed Martin

Main: http://www.lockheedmartin.com/
Career: http://www.lockheedmartinjobs.com/
HQ: 6801 Rockledge Dr., Bethesda, MD 20817
               Tel: +1 (301) 897-6000

Lockheed Martin is the world's largest defense and space company with operations in more than 500 cities across the United States and internationally in more than 70 nations and territories. With revenues in excess of $40 billion annually and more than 110,000 people worldwide, the firm is principally engaged in the research, design, development, manufacture, integration and sustainment of advanced technology systems, products and services. This includes satellites and technologies for communications, Earth observation and exploration, weather forecasting, planetary and asteroid exploration, and national security; launch vehicles; and ground operations support.

Major space facilities: Denver, CO; Colorado Springs, CO; Sunnyvale, CA; Palo Alto, CA; King of Prussia, PA; Newtown, PA; Huntsville, AL; Houston, TX; Cape Canaveral, FL; New Orleans, LA; Washington, DC-area.

Loral Space & Communications

Main:	http://www.loral.com
Career:	http://www.loral.com/careers/
HQ:	888 Seventh Ave., 40th Floor, New York, NY 10106
	Tel: +1 (212) 697-1105

Loral is a satellite communications company engaged, through ownership interests in affiliates, in satellite-based communications services.

Masten Space Systems

Main:	http://masten.aero/
Career:	http://masten.aero/company/careers/
HQ:	1570 Sabovich St., Mojave, CA 93501
	Tel: +1 (888) 488-8455

Masten Space Systems is a small, vertically-integrated aerospace R&D and flight services company creating and deploying reliable, reusable rocket vehicles and components. The company builds regeneratively cooled bipropellant propulsion systems and fully reusable vertical takeoff and landing launch vehicles. Masten focuses on unmanned suborbital flights.

MDA Corporation

Main:	http://www.mdacorporation.com
Career:	http://www.mdacorporation.com/corporate/careers/index.cfm
HQ:	Tel: +1 (604) 278-3411

MDA offers space-based solutions for direct-to-home television, satellite radio, broadband Internet, and mobile communications and surveillance and intelligence products that offer end-to-end solutions to monitor and manage changes and activities. Divisions manufacture communications satellites, and satellite antenna subsystems, electronics, and payloads; focus on robotics and automation; and perform geospatial analysis. The firm has 4,800 employees operating from 11 locations in the United States, Canada, and internationally.

SSL, A division of MDA

Main: http://www.ssloral.com/
HQ: 3825 Fabian Way, Palo Alto, CA 94303
             Tel: +1 (650) 852-4000

Formerly Space Systems/Loral, SSL is a leading manufacturer of commercial communications satellites to commercial customers across the globe. This business is located in Palo Alto, California, with offices in Pasadena, California, and Houston, Texas.

SSL Federal, LLC, A division of MDA

Main: http://www.sslfederal.com/

Offers all of MDA's Surveillance and Communications capability to U.S. government customers. Palo Alto, California, with an office in Chantilly, Virginia.

MDA Information Systems, LLC

Main: http://www.mdaus.com/
HQ: Suite 300 - 820 West Diamond Ave, Gaithersburg, MD 20878
             Tel: +1 (240) 833-8200

Offers geospatial information services derived from satellite data, as well as ground stations, to U.S. government customers.

MDA Satellite Subsystems

Main: http://www.mdacorporation.com/corporate/
             communications/communication_subsystems.cfm
HQ: 21025 Trans-Canada Hwy, Sainte-Anne-de-Bellevue, QC,
             Canada, H9X 3R2
             Tel: +1 (514) 457-2150

Satellite payloads, antenna and electronic subsystems, composite structures, and complete communications satellite solutions.

MDA Robotics and Automation

Main: http://www.mdacorporation.com/corporate/
             surveillance_intelligence/robotics_automation.cfm
HQ: 9445 Airport Road Brampton, ON, Canada, L6S 4J3
             Tel: +1 (905) 790-2800

MDA Geospatial Services
13800 Commerce Parkway Richmond, BC, Canada, V6V 2J3
Tel: +1 (604) 278-3411
http://gs.mdacorporation.com/

MDA Surveillance and Intelligence
13800 Commerce Parkway Richmond, BC, Canada, V6V 2J3
Tel: +1 (604) 278-341

MDA provides surveillance and intelligence systems and services that deliver operational information to support critical decision making for government, commercial and business customers. Solutions leverage data from space, airborne, maritime, ground and cyber sources to provide reliable, accurate, time-sensitive information that is embedded in our customers' business operations. MDA provides customers with two classes of solutions: turnkey operational system solutions and geospatial information services.

MIT Lincoln Laboratory
Main: http://www.ll.mit.edu/
Career: http://www.ll.mit.edu/college
HQ: 244 Wood St, Lexington, MA 02420-9108
         Tel: +1 (781) 981-5500

LLNL primary mission areas include: Space Control, communications systems, intelligence, surveillance, and reconnaissance systems, microelectronics, air traffic control and meteorology, and prototype engineering.

MOOG
Main: http://www.moog.com/
Space & Defense Group: http://www.moog.com/about/space-defense-group/
Career: http://www.moog.com/careers/
HQ: Jamison Road, East Aurora, New York 14052
         Tel: +1 (716) 652 2000
Moog Components Group
         1213 North Main Street, Blacksburg, VA 24060-3127

Moog supplies critical components, subsystems and systems to the launch vehicle and spacecraft markets. Our products position commercial and military satellites, position antennas, control propellant flow to and supply rocket engines, provide structures and vibration isolation, conduct communication on spacecraft through avionics, and steer launch and space vehicles.

Nanoracks LLC

Main: www.Nanoracks.com
HQ: 555 Forge River Road, Suite 120, Webster, TX 77598
        Tel: +1 (815) 425-8553

NanoRacks offers multiple commercial opportunities to use the U.S. National Lab on space station for education or industry research.

Northrop Grumman

Main: http://www.northropgrumman.com
Career: http://www.northropgrumman.com/careers/
HQ: 2980 Fairview Park Drive Falls Church, VA 22042
        Tel: +1 (703) 280-2900

Northrop Grumman Aerospace Systems

Main: http://www.northropgrumman.com/capabilities/space/Pages/default.aspx
HQ: One Space Park Redondo Beach, CA 90278
        Tel: +1 (310) 812-4321

Since the dawn of the space age, Northrop Grumman has put good ideas into orbit and beyond: systems engineering, spacecraft manufacturing, precision sensors, space instrument design, ground stations development and orbiting space platforms, propulsion systems, sensors, space science, earth observation/remote sensing, metrology and test equipment, satellite communications, and antennas.

Northrop Grumman Electronic Systems

HQ: 1580-A West Nursery Road Linthicum, Maryland 21090
        Tel: +1 (410) 765-1000

Northrop Grumman Electronic Systems manufactures, integrates and supports a variety of advanced electronic and maritime systems for U.S. and international customers for national security and non-defense applications. Systems include high performance sensors and intelligence processing and navigation systems operating in all environments from undersea to outer space. Applications include airborne surveillance, space sensing, biochemical detection, intelligence fusing and analysis, inertial navigation, air and missile defense, air traffic control, ship bridge control, communications.

Optimal Satcom

Main: http://www.optimalsatcom.com
HQ: 11180 Sunrise Valley Dr, Suite 200, Reston VA 20191
                     Tel: +1 (703) 657-8800

Provides enterprise systems, databases, and tools for satellite capacity planning, and VSAT network design and optimization.

Orbcomm

Main: http://www.orbcomm.com
Career: http://orbcomm.applicantstack.com/x/openings
HQ: 395 W Passaic Street, Suite 325, Rochelle Park, NJ 07662 USA
                     Tel: +1 (703) 433.6300
Innovation and Network Control Center:
                     22970 Indian Creek Drive, Suite 300, Sterling, VA 20166
                     Tel: +1 (703) 433.6300
Operations: 125 Business Park Drive, Suite 100, Utica, NY 13502
                     Tel: +1 (703) 433-6300

ORBCOMM's combination of global satellite and cellular services is a leading provider of global machine-to-machine (M2M) solutions and the only commercial satellite network 100 percent dedicated to M2M. Global M2M solutions are designed to track, monitor and control a variety of powered and unpowered assets in key vertical markets such as transportation and logistics, heavy equipment, oil and gas, maritime and government.

Orbital ATK

Main: http://www.orbitalatk.com
Careers: http://www.atk-jobs.com/
HQ: 45101 Warp Drive, Dulles, VA 20166
                     Phone: +1 (703) 406-5000

OrbitalATK has 3,400+ employees, with 1,700 engineers/scientists.
- Launch Vehicle Design and Manufacturing and Program Offices
  3380 South Price Rd., Chandler, AZ 85248
  Tel: +1 (480) 899-6000
- Satellite Design and Manufacturing
  1440 N. Fiesta Blvd., Gilbert, AZ 85233
  Tel: +1 (480) 892-8200

- Technical Services Division
  7500 Greenway Center Dr., Suite 700, Greenbelt, MD 20770
  Tel: +1 (301) 220-5600
- Southern California Engineering Center
  7711 Center Avenue, Suite 600, Huntington Beach, CA 92647
  Tel: +1 (714) 677-2428
- Missile Defense Systems Engineering and Manufacturing
  305A Quality Circle, Huntsville, AL 35806
  Tel: +1 (256) 971-0800
- Launch Vehicle Assembly, Test and Launch
  Building 1555 Talo Rd., Vandenberg AFB, CA 93437
  Tel: +1 (805) 734-5400

Wallops Island, Virginia—Launch Vehicle Assembly, Testing and Launch; Cargo Logistics Spacecraft Processing; Research Rocket Assembly, Test and Launch --
32421 Chincoteaque Road New Church, VA 23415

As the industry leader in small- and medium-class space and rocket systems, Orbital provides a complete set of reliable, cost-effective products.
Satellites include
- Geosynchronous-Earth Orbit (GEO) satellites for communications and broadcasting
- Low-Earth Orbit (LEO) spacecraft that perform remote sensing and scientific research
- Spacecraft used for national security missions
- Planetary probes to explore deep space

Launch vehicles include
- Rockets that transport satellites into orbit
- Missile defense interceptor booster vehicles deployed to protect against enemy missile attack
- Target rockets used to test missile defense systems

Paragon Space Development Company
Main: http://www.paragonsdc.com/
Career: http://www.paragonsdc.com/index.php?action=viewPost&postID=40
HQ: 3481 E. Michigan St., Tucson, AZ 85714
        Tel: +1 (520) 903-1000
        1322 Space Park Dr., Suite C150. Houston, TX 77058
        Tel: +1 (281) 957-9173

813 14th Street, Suite B. Golden, CO 80401
Tel: +1 (520) 981-2911

Paragon is the premier provider of environmental controls for extreme and hazardous environments. We design, build, test and operate premier life support systems and leading thermal control products for astronauts, contaminated water divers, and extreme environment adventurers, as well as for unmanned space and terrestrial applications.

Quintech Electronics

Main: http://www.quintechelectronics.com
HQ: 250 Airport Road, Indiana, PA 15701
Tel: +1 (724) 349-1412

Designs and manufactures RF signal management communications equipment for satellite, government, wireless, telecom, and broadcast customers.

Raytheon

Main: http://www.raytheon.com
Career: http://jobs.raytheon.com/
HQ: 870 Winter Street, Waltham, MA 02451-1449
        Tel: +1 (781) 522.3000

With 63,000 employees worldwide and more than $24 billion in sales, Raytheon is one of the world's largest defense contractors.

Space and Airborne Systems (El Segundo, CA; Goleta, CA; Annapolis Junction, MD). Builds radars and other sensors for aircraft, spacecraft and ships.

Missile Systems (Tucson, Arizona) Raytheon's space probes are designed to work faithfully for years in the extreme conditions of deep space or on other planets.

Raytheon Vision Systems (formerly Santa Barbara Research Center, CA) For more than 40 years provided the focal planes and sensors to the remote sensing scientific community for the investigation and characterization of Earth and other planets.

Other Locations: AL; AZ; CO; White Sands, NM; and VA.

Scaled Composites
Main:	http://www.scaled.com/about/
Careers:	http://www.scaled.com/careers/
HQ:	Hangar 78, Airport 1624 Flight Line, Mojave, CA 93501
	Tel: +1 (661) 824-4541

Founded in 1982 by Burt Rutan, Scaled has broad experience in air vehicle design, tooling and manufacturing, specialty composite structure design, analysis and fabrication, and developmental flight tests of air and space vehicles.

SES America
Main:	http://www.ses.com
Career:	http://www.ses.com/careers
HQ:	4 Research Way Princeton, NJ 08540-6684
	Tel: +1 (609) 987 4000
	1129 20th Street, N.W., Suite 1000, Washington, DC 20036
	Tel: +1 (202) 478-7100

SES U.S. Government Solutions
HQ:	11790 Sunrise Valley Drive, Suite 300, Reston, VA 20191
	Tel: +1 (703) 610-1000

A global satellite operator providing reliable and secure satellite communications solutions to broadcast, telecom, corporate and government customers worldwide, they own and operate a fleet of 53 geostationary satellites that are complemented by a network of teleports and offices located around the globe.

Sierra Nevada
Main:	http://www.sncorp.com/
Career:	https://careers.sncorp.com/
HQ:	444 Salomon Circle, Sparks, NV 89434
	Tel: +1 (775) 331-0222

Sierra Nevada Corporation's Space Systems
HQ:	1722 Boxelder Street, Suite 102, Louisville, CO 80027
	Tel: +1 (303) 530-1925

Orbital Technologies Corporation
www.orbitec.com
HQ:	1212 Fourier Drive, Madison, WI 53717
	Tel: +1 (608) 827-5000

SpaceDev, Inc. (California Division)
      http://www.spacedev.com
HQ: 13855 Stowe Drive, Poway, CA 92064
      Tel: +1 (858) 375-2000

MicroSat Systems, Inc.
      www.microsatsystems.com
HQ: 1722 Boxelder Street, Suite 102, Louisville, CO 80027
      Tel: +1 (303) 530-1925

SNC is a prime systems integrator and electronic systems provider. Since its founding in 1963, the company has focused on high-technology electronics, avionics, and communications systems. Renewable Energy, Telemedicine, Nanotechnology, Cyber, Net-Centric Operations, Microsatellites and Human Spaceflight. Our capabilities range from spacecraft actuators that power the Mars rovers, to hybrid rocket technologies that powered the first commercial astronaut to space, and from microsatellites controlled by the Internet to *Dream Chaser*, a winged and piloted orbital commercial spacecraft.

Four product lines include the following:

Spacecraft Systems provides small satellites to meet commercial, civil, and military mission requirements using common bus structures and components that are rapidly customized as needed for different mission applications.

Propulsion Systems offers safe, green, reliable and low-cost propulsion solutions for space vehicles, satellites and small to medium launch vehicle propulsion systems.

Space Exploration Systems is leading an effort to create a low-cost, safe commercial crew transportation service to and from low Earth orbit, including the International Space Station .

Space Technologies supplies critical components to such important national security programs as Advanced EHF, Mobile User Objective System, Space-Based Infrared System, and commercial imagery systems (GeoEye, Ikonos, Worldview). Spacecraft deployable systems, electrical power systems, thermal control systems, pointing systems and motion control, electronics, and mechanical and structural systems.

Sirius XM

Main: http://www.siriusxm.com/
Career: http://www.siriusxm.com/careers
HQ: 1221 Ave of the Americas, 36th floor, NY, NY 10020
             Tel: +1 (212) 584-5100

Sirius XM Holdings is a broadcasting company that provides two satellite radio services operating in the U.S., Sirius Satellite Radio and XM Satellite Radio. Sirius XM Canada, an affiliate company, provides service in Canada.

Southwest Research Institute

Main: http://www.swri.org/
Career: http://www.swri.org/HR/default.htm
HQ: 6220 Culebra Road, San Antonio, Texas 78228-0510
             Tel: +1 (210) 684-5111

SwRI's 10 technical divisions offer a wide range of technical expertise and services in such areas as chemistry, space science, nondestructive evaluation, automation, engine design, mechanical engineering, and electronics. For more than three decades, SwRI has been a recognized leader in space science research as well as in the development of spacecraft instrumentation, avionics and electronics for both government and industry. The Space Science and Engineering Division's scientific staff is active in a variety of research areas: heliospheric and solar physics; terrestrial and planetary magnetospheres; planetary geology and atmospheres; comets, asteroids, and other small solar system bodies; planetary system origins and formation; and high-energy astrophysics.

Space Adventures Ltd

Main: http://www.spaceadventures.com/
HQ: 8245 Boone Boulevard, Suite 570, Vienna, VA 22182
             Tel: +1 (703) 524.7172

Founded in 1998, Space Adventures is the world's premier private spaceflight company and the only company currently providing opportunities for actual private spaceflight and space tourism.

Space Dynamics Lab

Main: http://www.sdl.usu.edu/index
Careers: http://www.sdl.usu.edu/employment/
HQ: 1695 North Research Park Way, North Logan, Utah 84341
             Tel: +1 (435) 713-3400

SDL is a nonprofit research corporation and one of 14 University Affiliated Research Centers (UARCs) in the nation. Its core areas of expertise include: space-rated instruments and payloads, calibration; cryogenic and thermal management, small satellites and satellite systems; systems engineering, upper atmospheric measurements and modeling; sensor system performance modeling and simulation; data handling compression, and analysis; and ground stations and exploitation software. Field offices: Albuquerque, NM; Bedford, MA; Huntsville, AL; Houston, TX; Los Angeles, CA; Washington, DC.

Spaceport America
Main: http://www.spaceportamerica.com
HQ: 901 E University Ave, Suite 9652, Las Cruces, NM 88001
               Tel: +1 (575) 267-8500

Home to Virgin Galactic White Knight 2 and SpaceShip 2, Space X Falcon 9R, and suborbital launches.

SpaceQuest Ltd
Main: http://www.spacequest.com
HQ: 3554 Chain Bridge Road, Suite 103. Fairfax, VA 22030
               Tel: +1 (703) 424-7801

Provider of microsatellite technologies, systems and services

SpaceX
Main: http://www.spacex.com
Careers: http://www.spacex.com/careers
HQ: 1 Rocket Road Hawthorne, CA 90250
               Tel: +1 (310) 363-6000

SpaceX designs, manufactures and launches advanced rockets and spacecraft. The company was founded in 2002 to revolutionize space technology, with the ultimate goal of enabling people to live on other planets.

Surrey Satellite US LLC
Main: http://www.sst-us.com
US HQ: 345 Inverness Drive South, Suite 100, Englewood, CO 80112
               Tel: +1 (303) 790-0653

A wholly-owned subsidiary of a UK firm, the office was established in 2008 to address the U.S. market related to small satellite solutions, applications, and services. The firm has complete in-house capabilities to design, manufacture, launch, and operate small satellites focused on remote sensing, science, navigation, and telecommunications. The firm also offers space training and development programs.

Telesat

Main: http://www.telesat.com/
Career: http://www.telesat.com/about-us/careers
HQ: 1601 Telesat Court Ottawa, Ontario, Canada, K1B 5P4
                 Tel: +1 (613) 748-0123

Telesat is a leading global satellite communications operator with a fleet of more than a dozen satellites that provides solutions worldwide to broadcast, telecom, corporate and government customers. Telesat also manages the operations of satellites for third parties.

Trimble Navigation

Main: http://www.trimble.com
Careers: http://www.trimble.com/careers/
HQ: 935 Stewart Drive, Sunnyvale, CA 94085
                 Tel: +1 (408) 481-8000

Though best known for GPS technology, Trimble integrates a wide range of positioning technologies including GPS, laser, optical and inertial technologies with application software, wireless communications, and services to provide complete commercial solutions; serving a variety of industries including agriculture, engineering and construction, transportation and wireless communications infrastructure.

United Launch Alliance (ULA)

Main: http://www.ulalaunch.com/
Careers: http://www.ulalaunch.com/careers.aspx
Galileo Operations Center
                 9501 East Panorama Circle, Centennial, CO 80112
                 Tel: +1 (720) 922-7100

Formed in December 2006, United Launch Alliance is a 50–50 joint venture owned by Lockheed Martin and The Boeing Company. ULA brings together two of the launch industry's most experienced and successful teams—Atlas and Delta—to provide reliable, cost-efficient space launch services for the U.S. government. ULA program management, engineering, test, and mission support functions are headquartered in Denver, Colorado. Manufacturing, assembly and integration operations are located at Decatur, Alabama, and Harlingen, Texas. Launch operations are located at Cape Canaveral Air Force Station, Florida, and Vandenberg Air Force Base, California.

UTC Aerospace Systems

Main: http://www.utcaerospacesystems.com
Careers: http://www.utcaerospacesystemscareers.com/

Corporate: United Technologies 1 Financial Plaza, Hartford, CT 06103
                 Tel: +1 (860) 728-7000
HQ: UTC Aerospace Systems Four Coliseum Centre
                 2730 West Tyvola Road, Charlotte, NC 28217
                 Tel: +1 (450) 677-9411
ISR & Space Systems
                 7 Technology Park Dr., Westford, MA 01886-3141
SpaceSuits Engine Systems
                 1 Hamilton Road, Windsor Locks, CT 06096-1000
Attitude Determination Subsystem
                 100 Wooster Heights Road, Danbury, CT 06810–7589
                 Phone: +1 (203) 797-5210
SR Systems: 6600 Gulton Court, N.E., Albuquerque, NM 87109-4407
                 Tel +1 (505) 938-5096

UTC develops and produces advanced technologies for space and defense markets including products from space suits and undersea environmental systems to low-cost satellites and space telescope optics. The firm provides Environmental Control and Life Support Systems on the *International Space Station,* including the space suit; space and Mission Critical Electronics for data acquisition and command and control electronics for launch vehicle products including Command and data handling units, Data acquisition and management systems, Delay memory, Filter assemblies, Pre modulation signal conditioning, and Power regulation and distribution. Space capabilities and products include Tactical ISR Satellites; Electro-Optical Payloads; Precision Optics and Optical Subsystems; Actuation Systems; Launch Vehicle and Satellite Electronics. Space Attitude Control Sensors & Systems include Star trackers, Earth sensors, Magnetrometers, reaction control wheels, and Attitude determination and control interface.

Vacco Industries

Main: http://www.vacco.com
Careers: http://www.vacco.com/careers/overview
HQ: 10350 Vacco Street South, El Monte, CA 91733
                 Tel: +1 (626) 443-7121

VACCO Industries is a leading designer and manufacturer of specialty valves, filters and advanced fluid control products—offering innovative engineered solutions to critical missions for defense, space, and commercial markets.

Viasat

Main: http://www.viasat.com
Careers: https://www.viasat.com/careers
HQ: 6155 El Camino Real, Carlsbad, CA 92009
                 Tel: +1 (760) 476-2200
Comsat Labs: 20511 Seneca Meadows Parkway, Germantown, MD 20876
                 Tel: +1 (240) 686-4400
VSAT Networks: 725 Breckinridge Plaza, Duluth, GA 30096
                 Tel: +1 (678) 924-2400

ViaSat produces innovative satellite and other digital communications products that enable fast, secure, and efficient communications to any location. Products include satellite networks for fixed-site and mobile communications; satellite antenna systems; wireless datalinks and terminals for combat situational awareness; cybersecurity and information assurance for military networking and encrypted data storage; communication microprocessor chipsets; satellite network and RF system design; global mobile satellite services for aircraft, vehicles, and seagoing vessels; and satellite Internet access and other broadband services for consumers, business, and government.

Virgin Galactic

Main: http://www.virgingalactic.com/
Careers: https://careers-virgingalactic.icims.com/jobs/intro?branding=live

Virgin Galactic is comprised of hundreds of dedicated and passionate professionals—including rocket scientists, engineers, and designers from around the world—united in creating something new and lasting: the world's first commercial spaceline.

Wyle Laboratories

Main: http://www.wyle.com
Careers: http://www.wyle.com/careers.html
Science, Technology and Engineering Group HQ
                    1290 Hercules Ave,. Houston, TX 77058-2769
                    Tel: +1 (281) 212.1200

Wyle is a leading provider of specialized engineering, professional, scientific and technical services to the federal government with 4,000+ employees at 50-plus locations nationwide. The Science, Technology and Engineering Group provides innovative solutions for life sciences, pilot and health crew training and support, aerospace medicine, scientific services, and specialized engineering. Wyle experts have supported every U.S. manned space mission since the 1960s with expertise in specialized flight medicine services; astronaut/aircrew health and performance; climate prediction, atmospheric modeling and data sciences; life sciences with an emphasis on challenging environments such as micro-gravity of space, high-g and high altitude aircraft, medical systems engineering and integration; commercial spaceflight services; and spaceflight hardware production and certification

XCOR Aerospace

Main: http://www.xcor.com/
Careers: http://xcor.com/jobs/
HQ: PO Box 1163, Mojave CA, 93502
                    Tel: +1 (661) 824-4714

XCOR Aerospace is a small, privately-held California corporate focused on the research, development, project management, production and maintenance of safer, more reliable, reusable suborbital and orbital launch vehicles (RLVs), rocket engines and rocket propulsion systems.

X Prize Foundation

Main: www.xprize.org
Careers: http://www.xprize.org/about/careers
HQ: 800 Corporate Pointe, Suite 350, Culver City, CA 90230
                    Tel: +1 (310) 741-4880

Founded in 1995, XPRIZE is the leading organization solving the world's Grand Challenges by creating and managing large-scale, high-profile, incentivized prizes in five areas: Learning; Exploration; Energy & Environment; Global Development; and Life Sciences.

XTAR

Main:	http://xtar.com
HQ:	2551 Dulles View Drive, Suite 300, Herndon, VA 20171-5219
	Tel: +1 (571) 281-3570

A small commercial satellite operator exclusively providing services in the X-band frequency range, which is the communications cornerstone for military, diplomatic, humanitarian and emergency disaster response operations.

WORKING IN THE SPACE INDUSTRY

Biography & Advice

Name	Max Stolack
Organization	Pratt & Whitney
Job Title	Project Engineer, Rocket Engines
Location	West Palm Beach, Florida

Responsibilities
Our group is responsible for coordinating the activities of several departments involved with the manufacture, assembly, and test of experimental jet and rocket engines. One of our main responsibilities is troubleshooting problems so that the engine is built and tested properly, and is on-time and on-budget.

Degrees/School
B.S. Mechanical Engineering, Rensselaer Polytechnic Institute

Career Path
I thought about a career in robotics but shifted to rocket propulsion in my junior year. No direct job opportunity in space presented itself so I took a job working on jet engines before transferring internally to develop rocket engines for spaceflight.

Why Space?
You can see the big picture. When we take our engine to the test range and watch it work, we can see the results of our labor.

Words of Wisdom
Do not be afraid of changing jobs or careers. Space is made up of a range of organizations: big and small, private and government. Each person will find a different level of happiness in a different type of organization.

Appendix C: Canadian Organizations

In this appendix
Additional resources for people interested in opportunities in Canada.

Government

Canadian Space Agency
Government Established in March 1989, the Canadian Space Agency (CSA) was created through an Act of Parliament to meet the needs of Canadians for scientific knowledge, space technology and information. Overall, the CSA has about 670 employees with approximately 90 percent of them employed at the John H. Chapman Space Centre, the agency's headquarters. CSA directs its resources and activities through four key programs:

Earth Observation   Space Science and Exploration
Satellite Communications   Space Awareness

> John H. Chapman Space Centre
> 6767 Route de l'Aéroport
> Saint-Hubert, Quebec J3Y 8Y9 Canada
> Tel: +1 (450) 926-4800
> Website: http://www.asc-csa.gc.ca/eng
> Career: http://www.esdc.gc.ca/en/jobs/index.page

David Florida Laboratory
The David Florida Laboratory (DFL) is Canada's world-class spacecraft assembly, integration and testing center located in Ottawa. On a fee-for-service basis, the DFL is available for use by Canadian and foreign aerospace and telecommunications companies and organizations for qualifying hardware. It is registered as ISO 9001:2008 for radio frequency, structural, and thermal qualification testing of space bound and terrestrial hardware. Support facilities include offices, conference rooms, storage areas, check-out rooms, and inhouse mechanical, electrical and electronic shops.

3701 Carling Avenue
P.O. Box 11490, Station H
Ottawa, Ontario K2H 8S2 Canada
Tel: +1 (613) 998-2383
http://www.asc-csa.gc.ca/eng/dfl/

Universities and Institutions

Canadian Aeronautics and Space Institute

The Canadian Aeronautics and Space Institute is a nonprofit professional scientific and technical organization devoted to the advancement of the art, science and engineering of aeronautics, astronautics and associated technologies in Canada. CASI holds conferences, workshops, and symposia; and sponsors the Charles Luttman and Elvie L. Smith scholarships.

350 Terry Fox Drive, Suite 104
Kanata, Ontario K2K 2W5 Canada
Tel: +1 (613) 591-8787
http://www.casi.ca/

McGill University Institute of Air & Space Law

For more than 50 years, the institute has been offering an intensive program of graduate studies in international and comparative air law and, since 1957, in the law of space applications. More than 800 students from over 120 different countries successfully completed their graduate studies and obtained the Graduate Certificate in Air and Space Law (originally Diploma in Air and Space Law), the Master of Laws (LL.M.) degree, or the Doctor of Civil Law (DCL) degree.

3690 Peel Street
Montreal, Quebec H3A 1Q9 Canada
Tel.: +1 (514) 398-5095
http://www.mcgill.ca/iasl/institute-air-and-space-law

Ryerson University: Aerospace Engineering
Offers masters and PhD programs in aerospace engineering

> 245 Church Street (at Gould Street)
> Toronto, Ontario M5B 2K3 Canada
> Tel: +1 (416) 979-5000, ext. 2790
> http://www.ryerson.ca/graduate/aerospace/

University of Calgary: Institute for Space Imaging Science
Research in space plasma, auroral imaging, analysis, and modeling.

> 2500 University Drive NW
> Calgary, Alberta T2N 1N4 Canada
> Tel:+1 (403) 220-5385
> http://www.phys.ucalgary.ca/

York University Lassonde School of Engineering
Offers the only space science program in Canada providing courses to students interested in a career in spacecraft design, scientific design, space exploration, space and satellite technology, or in the study of the atmosphere through the use of satellites, rockets, and other space vehicles. The school also offers a bachelor of engineering degree that will train in the technologies used in satellite and space missions while providing a grounding in applied mathematics, physics, and computer sciences.

> http://futurestudents.yorku.ca/program/space_engineering
> http://futurestudents.yorku.ca/program/space_science

The school's Space Engineering Laboratory reproduces on a scale suitable for a university environment all of the infrastructure necessary for the end-to-end design, development, manufacture, test, operation and disposal of space systems including spacecraft, probes, landers and rovers.

> 4700 Keele Street
> Toronto, Ontario M3J 1P3 Canada
> Tel: +1 (416) 736-2100
> http://www.yorku.ca/bquine/default.htm

Associations / Organizations

Aerospace Industries Association of Canada

A nonprofit that advocates aerospace policy in Canada

> 225 Albert Street, Suite 703
> Ottawa, ONT K1P 6A9 Canada
> Tel: +1 (613) 232-4297
> http://www.aiac.ca

Canadian Space Commerce Association

Hosts a number of networking events.

> Toronto Street, Suite #458
> Toronto, Ontario M5C 2B5 Canada
> Tel: +1 (647) 985-9203
> http://spacecommerce.ca/

Canadian Space Society

A nonprofit organization of professionals and enthusiasts pursuing the human exploration and development of the solar system and beyond via technical and outreach projects.

> 1115 Lodestar Road, Bldg E, PO Box 70009, Rimrock Plaza
> Toronto, Ontario M3J 0H3 Canada
> http://www.css.ca

Appendix D: Astronomy and Astrophysics Programs

In this appendix
The American Astronomical Society's list of astronomy degree-granting institutions.

Institution	City, State	Website Address
Agnes Scott College	Decatur, GA	http://www.agnesscott.edu/physics/
University of Alabama	Huntsville, AL	http://www.uah.edu/science/departments/physics
University of Alabama	Tuscaloosa, AL	http://astronomy.ua.edu/
University of Arizona	Tucson, AZ	https://www.as.arizona.edu
Arizona State University	Tempe, AZ	http://sese.asu.edu/
Barnard College	New York, NY	http://www.phys.barnard.edu/
Boston University	Boston, MA	http://www.bu.edu/astronomy/
University of California	Berkeley, CA	http://astro.berkeley.edu/
University of California	Los Angeles, CA	http://www.astro.ucla.edu/
University of California	LaJolla, CA	http://casswww.ucsd.edu/index.php/Main_Page
University of California	Santa Cruz, CA	http://www.astro.ucsc.edu/
California Institute of Technology	Pasadena, CA	http://www.astro.caltech.edu/
Calvin College	Grand Rapids, MI	http://www.calvin.edu/academic/phys/
Case Western Reserve University	Cleveland, OH	http://astronomy.case.edu/
University of Central Florida	Orlando, FL	http://planets.ucf.edu/
College of Charleston	Charleston, SC	http://physics.cofc.edu/
University of Chicago	Chicago, IL	http://astro.uchicago.edu/
Colgate University	Hamilton, NY	http://departments.colgate.edu/physics/
University of Colorado	Boulder, CO	http://aps.colorado.edu/
Columbia University	New York, NY	http://www.astro.columbia.edu/
Cornell University	Ithaca, NY	www.astro.cornell.edu
Dartmouth College	Hanover, NH	http://physics.dartmouth.edu/

University of Delaware	Newark, DE	http://web.physics.udel.edu/
University of Denver	Denver, CO	http://www.du.edu/nsm/departments/phy sicsandastronomy
University of Florida	Gainesville, FL	http://www.astro.ufl.edu/
Florida Institute of Technology	Melbourne, FL	http://cos.fit.edu/pss/
Franklin and Marshall College	Lancaster, PA	http://www.fandm.edu/physics/astronom y
University of Georgia	Athens, GA	http://www.physast.uga.edu/
Georgia State University	Atlanta, GA	http://phy-astr.gsu.edu
Goucher College	Towson, MD	http://www.goucher.edu/academics/phys ics-and-astronomy
Harvard University	Cambridge, MA	http://astronomy.fas.harvard.edu/
Haverford College	Haverford, PA	http://www.haverford.edu/physics-astro
University of Hawaii	Honolulu, HI	http://www.ifa.hawaii.edu/
University of Hawaii at Hilo	Hilo, HI	http://www.astro.uhh.hawaii.edu/
Howard University	Washington, DC	http://www.physics1.howard.edu/
University of Illinois	Urbana, IL	http://www.astro.illinois.edu/
Indiana University	Bloomington, IN	http://www.astro.indiana.edu/
University of Iowa	Iowa City,, IA	http://www.physics.uiowa.edu/
Iowa State University	Ames, IA	http://www.physastro.iastate.edu/
Johns Hopkins University	Baltimore, MD	http://physics-astronomy.jhu.edu/
University of Kansas	Lawrence, KS	http://www.physics.ku.edu/
Kansas State University	Manhattan, KS	https://www.phys.ksu.edu/
Lehigh University	Bethlehem, PA	http://physics.cas2.lehigh.edu/
Louisiana State University	Baton Rouge, LA	http://www.phys.lsu.edu/newwebsite/
University of Louisville	Crestwood, KY	http://www.astro.louisville.edu/
Lycoming College	Williamsport, PA	http://www.lycoming.edu/astronomy/
University of Maine	Orono, ME	http://www.physics.umaine.edu/
University of Maryland	College Park, MD	http://www.astro.umd.edu/
University of Maryland Baltimore	Baltimore, MD	http://physics.umbc.edu/
MIT	Cambridge, MA	http://web.mit.edu/physics/
University of Michigan, Ann Arbor	Ann Arbor, MI	http://www.lsa.umich.edu/astro/

Michigan State University	East Lansing, MI	http://www.pa.msu.edu/astro/Astronomy.html
University of Minnesota	Minneapolis, MN	http://www.astro.umn.edu/
Minnesota State University	Moorhead, MN	http://physics.mnstate.edu/index.html
University of Missouri at Columbia	Columbia, MO	http://physics.missouri.edu/
Montana State University	Bozeman, MT	http://www.physics.montana.edu/
University of Nebraska	Lincoln, NE	http://www.unl.edu/physics/
University of New Mexico	Albuquerque, NM	http://physics.unm.edu/
New Mexico Institute of Mining and Technology	Socorro, NM	http://physics.nmt.edu/
New Mexico State University	Las Cruces, NM	http://astronomy.nmsu.edu/dept/html/facade.html
University of North Carolina	Chapel Hill, NC	http://physics.unc.edu/
Northwestern University	Evanston, IL	http://www.physics.northwestern.edu/
Ohio State University	Columbus, OH	http://astronomy.osu.edu/
Ohio University	Athens, OH	http://www.ohio.edu/cas/physastro/
University of Oklahoma	Norman, OK	http://www.nhn.ou.edu/
Penn State University	University Park, PA	http://astro.psu.edu/
University of Pennsylvania	Philadelphia, PA	http://www.physics.upenn.edu/
University of Pittsburgh	Pittsburgh, PA	http://www.phyast.pitt.edu/
Pomona College	Claremont, CA	http://astronomy.pomona.edu/
Princeton University	Princeton, NJ	http://www.princeton.edu/astro/
Purdue University	West Lafayette, IN	http://www.astro.purdue.edu/
Rensselaer Polytechnic Institute	Troy, NY	http://www.rpi.edu/dept/phys/
Rice University	Houston, TX	http://www.physics.rice.edu/
University of Rochester	Rochester, NY	http://www.pas.rochester.edu/
Rochester Institute of Technology	Rochester, NY	http://www.rit.edu/cos/physics/
Rutgers University	Piscataway,NJ	http://www.physics.rutgers.edu/
San Diego State University	San Diego, CA	http://mintaka.sdsu.edu/
San Francisco State University	San Francisco, CA	http://www.physics.sfsu.edu/
St. Cloud State University	St. Cloud, MN	http://www.stcloudstate.edu/physics/

Smith College	Northampton, MA	http://www.smith.edu/astronomy/
Stanford University	Stanford, CA	https://physics.stanford.edu/
Stony Brook University	Stony Brook, NY	http://www.astro.sunysb.edu/astro/
Swarthmore College	Swarthmore, PA	http://www.swarthmore.edu/physics-astronomy
University of Texas at Austin	Austin, TX	http://www.as.utexas.edu/
Texas A&M University	College Station, TX	http://physics.tamu.edu/
Texas Christian University	Fort Worth, TX	http://www.phys.tcu.edu/
Texas Tech University	Lubbock, TX	http://www.phys.ttu.edu/
University of Toledo	Toledo, OH	http://www.utoledo.edu/nsm/physast/
Tufts University	Medford, MA	http://sites.tufts.edu/physics/
University of Utah	Salt Lake City, UT	http://www.physics.utah.edu/
Vanderbilt University	Nashville, TN	http://www.vanderbilt.edu/physics/index.php
Vassar College	Poughkeepsie, NY	http://physicsandastronomy.vassar.edu/
Villanova University	Villanova, PA	http://www.astronomy.villanova.edu/
University of Virginia	Charlottesville, VA	http://www.astro.virginia.edu/
Virginia Tech	Blacksburg, VA	http://www.phys.vt.edu/
University of Washington	Seattle, WA	http://www.astro.washington.edu/
Washington State University	Pullman, WA	http://www.physics.wsu.edu/
Washington University in St. Louis	St. Louis, MO	http://www.physics.wustl.edu/
Wellesley College	Wellesley, MA	http://www.wellesley.edu/Astronomy
Wesleyan University	Middletown, CT	http://www.wesleyan.edu/astro/
Whitman College	Walla Walla, WA	http://www.whitman.edu/academics/departments-and-programs/astronomy
Williams College	Williamstown, MA	http://astronomy.williams.edu/
University of Wisconsin	Madison, WI	www.astro.wisc.edu
University of Wyoming	Laramie, WY	www.uwyo.edu/physics/
Yale University	New Haven, CT	www.astro.yale.edu/
Youngstown State University	Youngstown, OH	http://web.ysu.edu/stem/physics/

INDEX

A quick guide to finding what you are looking for.

WORKING IN THE SPACE INDUSTRY

Biography & Advice

Name	Elizabeth Silbolboro Mezzacappa
Organization	Columbia–Presbyterian Medical Center
Job Title	Psychological Researcher
Location	New York City, NY

Responsibilities
Psychological Research

Degrees/School
B.A. Psychology and Biology, University of Pennsylvania
PhD Medical Psychology, Uniformed Services University of the Health Sciences
Life Sciences Program, International Space University

Career Path
I am a space medical psychologist working among the space, academic, and lay communities. While I am not in daily contact with space medical and psychological research, I see it as part of my responsibility to inform these communities through my participation in invited workshops, lectures, and presentations on psychological aspects of living in space. For example, I founded the Aerospace Biomedical Association at my university and have presented research relating to space at the Ford Foundation/National Academy of Sciences meeting and the annual convention of the American Psychological Society. My Ph.D. work was supported by a NASA Graduate Student Researchers Fellowship award. Early last year, I was awarded a small grant from the 2111 Foundation for Exploration to investigate cloistered contemplative communities as psychosocial space analogs.

Why Space?
Human psychological and behavioral issues are perhaps the least examined, yet arguably the most important for a permanent exodus into space.

Words of Wisdom
You don't have to be "in" the space community per se, to make a contribution to the space effort in psychology. One can do meaningful space psychological research outside of NASA or the space industry. There is so much to be done, it can't be restricted to the typical spaceflight centers.

(Biography & Advice)

Name   Jason Townsend
Organization   NASA
Job Title   Deputy Social Media Manager
Location   Washington, DC
Link   www.nasa.gov

Responsibilities

As the Deputy Social Media Manager for NASA, I help oversee and coordinate nearly 500 social media accounts covering NASA's people, missions, and programs
across 12 different platforms. I routinely coordinate between internal social media
users and NASA's external community of fans and followers to tell NASA's story
using tools such as the agency's flagship Twitter account, @NASA, Instagram
account, and pages on Facebook and Google+. I also provide guidance to agency
leadership on social media best practices, policy, and upcoming social media activities. Additionally, I am responsible for NASA Socials; events that take online
engagement with fans and followers to the next level through behind-the-scenes, in-
person experiences at NASA.

Degrees/School

B.A. Political Science, University of Colorado at Boulder

Career Path

I have over 15 years of professional and freelance experience communicating online,
starting as a freelance web designer for small local businesses and student organizations at colleges and universities in 1999.

I began fulltime summer employment as an intern at NASA's Goddard Space Flight
Center where I worked on building web pages and engaged in other activities for the
public affairs office. That internship grew to include year-around employment part-
time while continuing to go to school and continued fulltime during school breaks for
the remainder of my undergraduate years. Upon graduation, NASA was not hiring in
my field, so I took a job at the Department of Education coordinating a network of
websites and web applications for special education teachers around the country.
Later, I returned to NASA where I was a contractor at NASA Headquarters working
as an editor and producer for the NASA.gov website. During my time working on the
website, I was also involved in supporting the growing presence NASA had on social
media. After a few years in this role, I had an opportunity to take a civil service position at the National Oceanic and Atmospheric Administration as their webmaster. At
NOAA, I specialized in the creation, development and operations of online commu-

nications for NOAA.gov and NOAA's social media accounts. And that led me to my current job at NASA.

Why Space?

I was obsessed with science fiction, *Star Trek* in particular, as a kid. It still captures my imagination to this day. And I have come to realize that deep down, everyone has some sort of childlike wonderment in them like that. For many, it's the moments where they look at the stars in the night sky and wonder what's out there. Being able to help keep that sense of wonderment alive by sharing the story of what is really out there and how it is being explored is just an incredible opportunity that makes me excited to go to work each day. I've left jobs at NASA twice and returned twice. Each time, I realize this is what I want to do with my life. I want to share space with the world and engage humanity about the world around them, while telling the story of incredible discoveries and technical triumphs that allow us to be a species of explorers.

Words of Wisdom

One of the biggest pieces of advice I give students all the time is to take advantage of an internship opportunity while they are still in school. It is essential at building experience that can be essential in landing your first fulltime job out of school. My internship at NASA Goddard was invaluable at building a network of contacts and a body of experience that continues to propel me throughout my career.

Comments, Suggestions, Improvements

Have you learned something in your job search that you would like to share with others?

Have you come across information that you believe we should include in future editions?

Do you have changes to material presented in this book?

Perhaps you would like to send a note letting us know how you used this book.

We would like to hear from you.

Space Careers
PO Box 5752
Bethesda, MD 20824-5752
United States
careers@spacebusiness.com
www.spacebusiness.com/careers

Want more space?
Check out www.spacehistory101.com

Made in the USA
Lexington, KY
15 February 2017